Reading Comprehension Acro...

Grade 7

Mrs. Bazner

Contents

Graphic Organizers

Reading Comprehension Across the Genres

A Simple, Flexible Solution for Reading Skills Support

Homework

Assign meaningful, student-centered homework that can be completed in a single sitting.

Practice

Assign independent practice for core reading skills.

Enrichment

Provide students with opportunities for deeper study.

Remediation

Target certain text types or skills that need further attention.

Reinforcement/ Review

Support and review key topics from your curriculum.

Reading Comprehension Across the Genres 7, SV 1419023624

Core Reading Skills Instruction

Reading Comprehension Across the Genres provides activity-based instruction for the reading skills that matter most, including . . .

- Identifying main idea and supporting details
- Analyzing author's purpose
- Making inferences
- Drawing conclusions
- Understanding a text's key features
- Making connections to other texts and to the real world
- Extending the text into writing and speaking

Wide Exposure to Genres

Reading Comprehension Across the Genres helps students master core reading skills while providing important exposure to a wide **variety of genres, or text types**, including . . .

- essays
- novels
- letters
- reviews
- cartoons
- poems
- scripts
- journals
- short stories
- advertisements
- functional documents
- tables and charts

Clear, Student-Friendly Lessons

Each lesson in *Reading Comprehension Across the Genres* begins with a **short reading selection** followed by **five exercises**.

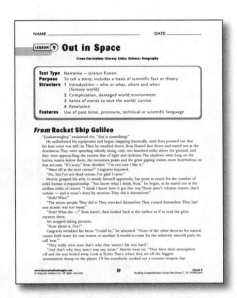

Before Reading

Students are introduced to the important aspects of the text, including its type, purpose, structure, and core features.

After Reading

Students complete five exercises that provide careful, student-friendly guidance in understanding the text.

5-Step Exercise Format

The carefully designed exercise format guides students step-by-step through the lessons—taking students from basic understanding to complete comprehension!

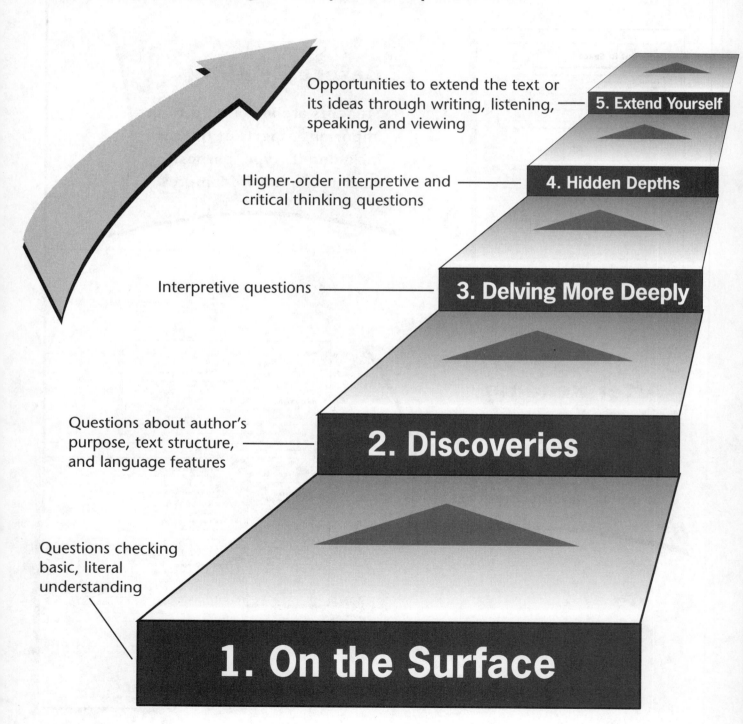

Opportunities to extend the text or its ideas through writing, listening, speaking, and viewing — **5. Extend Yourself**

Higher-order interpretive and critical thinking questions — **4. Hidden Depths**

Interpretive questions — **3. Delving More Deeply**

Questions about author's purpose, text structure, and language features — **2. Discoveries**

Questions checking basic, literal understanding — **1. On the Surface**

Correlation to Genres

Genre or Text Type	Lesson
Informative Nonfiction	3, 8, 14, 17, 24, 25
Narrative Fiction	1, 9, 12, 18, 27
Persuasive/Analytical Documents	11, 20, 22, 30
Functional Documents	5, 7, 10, 15, 16, 19, 21, 26, 29, 32, 34, 35
Formal Letters	4, 33
E-Communications	28
Poetry	13
Scripts/Dramas	6, 31
Journals	2
Cartoons	23

Cross-Curriculum Literacy Links

Curriculum Area	Lesson
Arts	5, 6, 11, 13, 18, 29, 30, 31
Civics and Citizenship	1, 3, 4, 10, 15, 20, 21, 22, 23, 24, 27, 28, 30, 32, 33
Difference and Diversity	12, 23, 25
Gender	25
Geography	2, 4, 5, 9, 15, 16, 17, 27, 34, 35
Health	19, 25, 34, 35
History	2, 3, 5, 10, 14, 18, 21, 23, 24, 31
Mathematics	16, 17, 26, 35
Multicultural Content	2, 4, 28, 34, 35
Science	5, 7, 8, 9, 10, 15, 16, 17, 20, 22
Work, Employment, and Enterprise	18, 31, 33

 **The Deputy Principal**

Cross-Curriculum Literacy Links: Civics and Citizenship

Text Type	Narrative
Purpose	To tell a story
Structure	1 Introduction — who or what, where and when
	2 Complication
	3 Series of events
	4 Resolution
Features	Use of past tense and pronouns

From Crossfire

The Deputy Principal scurried along the corridor, his leather shoes pounding the old wooden floorboards like hammers. Two unhappy boys, heads down and shoulders hunched, hurried to stay in his wake. As the little procession passed each classroom, heads were lowered again, like animals in a field returning to their quiet grazing. When they reached the bank of grey metal lockers, the marchers halted and the Deputy Principal said simply, "Aldridge, I want you to get out your guitar case."

Luke Aldridge stepped forward. Though only fourteen, he was almost as tall as the Deputy Principal, but whereas the Deputy was a ball of a man, with muscular arms and legs and a head that seemed to sit on his shoulders without need of a neck, Luke was slim and angular. His movements were awkward; he hadn't yet learned to control his rapidly growing body. And now he was nervous, which made his movements even more clumsy as he worked the dial of the combination lock. It fell open, and as instructed he withdrew a black guitar case, ancient and battered, made from the rigid cardboard used before vinyl and plastic became available. It was secured by two catches speckled with rust.

"Open it," commanded the Deputy Principal.

"It's locked and I don't have the key," Luke said.

"Don't give me that! This is your case isn't it?"

But the Deputy was deprived his full measure of anger when the second boy interrupted, digging into his pocket.

"I have the key, Sir."

"Is that so? Interesting. Well then, you open it, Tertzowjic." He pronounced the name perfectly and couldn't resist a satisfied smile to himself at the evident surprise this confident performance produced. Most who confronted this name balked and stammered their way through it.

The second boy, who now held the tiny key in his hand, took the guitar case from his companion and placed it carefully on the floor. Kneeling beside it, he inserted the key in each lock in turn, then released both spring-loaded latches together, with a "flick-thud" sound. The boy hesitated then, head bowed, and a second later the Deputy Principal denied him the dubious honour of raising the lid. Instead, he hooked the toe of his shoe under the rim and flipped it upwards.

9

All three stood gazing at the contents without the least surprise. After all, why should there be any surprise? The two boys had both known exactly what was inside and the Deputy Principal had certainly expected to see what lay before him now. That was why this little melodrama was being played out.

from *Crossfire* by James Maloney. Brisbane: University of Queensland Press, 1992. Pp. 1–2.

On the Surface

1 Who is in trouble with the Deputy Principal? _____

2 In whose locker is the guitar case? _____

3 Why can't Luke open the guitar case? _____

4 Why weren't any of them surprised at what was in the case? _____

_____

Discoveries

1 Write the meanings of the following words.

   a principal (adj.) _____

   b principal (noun) _____

   c melodrama _____

   d balked _____

   e dubious _____

   f scurried _____

   g hunched _____

2 Similes are comparisons which use the words *like* or *as*, e.g., "It was light as day." Give two examples of simile from the passage.

_____

_____

3 Would this melodrama have been as effective if the Deputy Principal had told the boys what he knew before he marched them down to their lockers? Why or why not?

_____

_____

Reading Comprehension Across the Genres 7, SV 1419023624

Delving More Deeply

1   What do the students in the classrooms do when the procession passes their room?

_____

2   Think about how the characters are described in the passage. With whom do you think the writer's sympathy lies: the boys or the Deputy Principal?

_____

_____

3   Can we assume that the guitar case belongs to Aldridge? _____

_____

_____

4   How do we know the boys are worried about what the Deputy Principal is about to find in the case?

_____

_____

5   Why do you think the Deputy Principal opens the case with his foot? _____

_____

_____

Hidden Depths

1   The guitar case obviously does not contain a guitar. What do you think is in the case?

_____

_____

2   The Deputy Principal seems to be pleased that he has caught the boys. What do you think his attitude is toward the boys?

_____

_____

Extend Yourself

•   Script the conversation between the Deputy Principal and the person who informed on the boys.

•   Write the next scene in the story. What is in the guitar case?

•   Sketch the scene based on the descriptions in this text.

•   Present a role play of this passage to the class.

LESSON 2 To Castle Dracula

Cross-Curriculum Literacy Links: History; Geography; Multicultural Content

Text Type	Journal or diary
Purpose	To reconstruct past experiences by telling events in the order in which they occurred
Structure	1 Introduction — background information telling who, where, and when
	2 Series of events in chronological order
	3 A personal comment
Features	Abbreviations, informal language, varied sentences, personal reflections

Jonathan Harker's Journal

3 May. Bistritz. — Left Munich at 8.35 P.M., on 1st May, arriving at Vienna early next morning; should have arrived at 6:46, but train was an hour late. Buda-Pesth seems a wonderful place, from the glimpse which I got of it from the train and the little I could walk through the streets. I feared to go very far from the station, as we had arrived late and would start as near the correct time as possible. The impression I had was that we were leaving the West and entering the East; the most Western of splendid bridges over the Danube, which is here of noble width and depth, took us among the traditions of Turkish rule.

We left in pretty good time, and came after nightfall to Klausenburgh. Here I stopped for the night at the Hotel Royale. I had for dinner, or rather supper, a chicken done up some way with red pepper, which was good but thirsty. (*Mem.,* get recipe for Mina.)

I asked the waiter, and he said it was called "paprika hendl," and that, as it was a national dish, I should be able to get it anywhere along the Carpathians. I found my smattering of German very useful here; indeed, I don't know how I should be able to get on without it.

Having some time at my disposal when in London, I had visited the British Museum, and made search among the books and maps in the library regarding Transylvania; it had struck me that some foreknowledge of the country could hardly fail to have some importance in dealing with a noble of that country. I find that the district he named is in the extreme east of the country, just on the borders of three states, Transylvania, Moldavia, and Bukovina, in the midst of the Carpathian mountains; one of the wildest and least known portions of Europe. I was not able to light on any map or work giving the exact locality of the Castle Dracula, as there are no maps of this country as yet to compare with our own Ordnance Survey maps; but I found that Bistritz, the post town named by Count Dracula, is a fairly well-known place.

from *Dracula* by Bram Stoker. London: Penguin, 1993. Pp. 7–8.

On the Surface

1 Between what two cities is Jonathan Harker traveling? _____

_____

2 At what time and on what date did Jonathan leave Munich? _____

_____

3 What form or mode of transport was Jonathan using? _____

_____

4 What are the main ingredients of "paprika hendl"? _____

_____

5 What does Jonathan note to himself as a reminder? Circle the answer.

    a To get "paprika hendl" in the Carpathians

    b To get a recipe for Mina

    c To get a map showing Castle Dracula

Discoveries

1 Locate and highlight or underline examples of abbreviation (shortened forms representing words) used in this text. Share and discuss.

2 Find synonyms (words with the same or similar meanings) for these words as they are used in this text.

    a glimpse _____

    b impression _____

    c splendid _____

    d nightfall _____

    e thirsty _____

    f time at my disposal _____

    g smattering _____

    h extreme _____

Delving More Deeply

1 Jonathan is able to speak at least two languages. What are they? _____

_____

2 Why is Jonathan traveling to Bistritz? Circle the answer.

   a For a holiday

   b To experience different cultures

   c To meet Count Dracula

3 How has Jonathan tried to prepare for his journey and meeting? _____

_____

4 List clues that indicate this diary is not set in modern times. _____

_____

_____

Hidden Depths

1 Who do you think Mina could be? Give reasons. _____

_____

_____

2 How do you think Jonathan Harker was feeling during this journey? Justify your answer.

_____

_____

_____

Extend Yourself

• Investigate the history and legend of Dracula and write a short report.

• Use the entertainment guide in a newspaper to research the types or genres of films currently being shown at cinemas. What proportion of current films could be classified as horror films or thrillers?

• Investigate why readers and viewers enjoy the horror genre. Write a bulleted summary of your findings.

LESSON 3 Growing Up

Cross-Curriculum Literacy Links: History; Civics and Citizenship

Text Type	Account
Purpose	To reconstruct past experiences by telling events in the order in which they occurred
Structure	1 Introduction — background information about who, where, and when
	2 Series of events in chronological order
	3 Personal comment (optional)
Features	Use of past tense, action verbs, descriptive language; may include quotes

From "My Dad"

My dad had just turned seven. He lived on a mission about twenty minutes' walk from the farm where nearly everyone from the mission worked. While the adults worked the children played in the fields, chasing mice, rabbits, birds etc.

One day while they were playing a truck came into the driveway and stopped outside the house. Everyone was curious about what the truck was there for, then when the driver and the farmer headed towards the field where my dad and his cousins were playing, all the children became scared. They didn't know why, but it was the look on the men's faces.

When they reached the children the farmer pointed to my dad and his cousin, Djalanga. The driver seized the two by the arms and dragged them away behind him. My dad was hitting, biting and kicking this man, as was his cousin. Neither of them knew what was happening but the sight of their mothers screaming and crying, struggling to reach them, had both boys terrified. They were pushed into the back of the truck and the doors were closed. Just before they closed my father saw my grandmother crying and clutching her chest. This was the last my father saw of my grandmother for fifteen years.

He was taken to a home for Aboriginal children who were considered "white enough" to go to school and have an education. My dad took this opportunity and finished high school, topping the school. His life at the home was very miserable and cruel. He was often beaten for not forgetting that he had a family. Once he was locked in a cupboard for three days with no food or water, for wanting his mother when he was sick.

On his twenty-second birthday my father received a card from his uncle who lived in the same suburb. He then discovered that my grandmother had moved to Sydney, so he moved to Sydney to be with her. This experience shaped my father into the person he is now. At the home he was punished because he wouldn't conform. He didn't accept "their" ways then and he won't accept them now.

from "My Dad" by Kathleen Priest, in *Nothing Interesting About Cross St.*,
Ed. Beth Yahp. Sydney: Angus & Robertson, 1996. P. 43.

On the Surface

1 Where did the adults on the mission work? _____

_____

2 How did they get to work? _____

_____

3 List the family members who were at the farm the day the boys were taken. _____

_____

4 How did the two boys, and their relatives, react to their being taken? _____

_____

5 What kind of home was one of the boys taken to? _____

_____

_____

Discoveries

1 Aboriginal peoples in Australia were once treated badly, as Native American peoples sometimes were in the United States. What terrible thing happens to the author's father because he is Aboriginal?

_____

_____

2 Find out the meaning of "assimilation"; then write a sentence explaining how it relates to the story.

_____

_____

_____

Delving More Deeply

1 Why were the boys terrified? _____

_____

_____

2 Why did all the children become scared when they saw the men in the truck?

_____

3 What did the people at the home want the boy to forget? _____

_____

4 How did the boy respond to this "opportunity" to have an education? _____

_____

Hidden Depths

1 How do you think the young boy would have felt on arriving at the home? Try to think of at least five adjectives.

_____

_____

2 What sort of education do you think the boys would have been given on the mission?

_____

_____

_____

Extend Yourself

• Research life on a modern Native American reservation, the equivalent of an Australian "mission." Present your findings to the class.

• Interview a member of your own family about his or her past. Write an account of the experiences.

• Write a short opinion piece: Should the government have to apologize to the author's father? What should the apology say?

LESSON (4) Dear Editor

Cross-Curriculum Literacy Links: Geography; Civics and Citizenship; Multicultural Content

Text Type	Letter to the editor
Purpose	To communicate information, experiences or ideas, formally or informally, in writing to a reader who is not present
Structure	1 Address and date
	2 Greeting
	3 Series of events or issues in paragraphs
	4 Name of writer
Features	Set layout, informal or formal language depending on purpose and audience, varied sentences

Make Sure Money Goes to the Victims

April 16, 2005

Dear Sir,

News of the devastating tsunami that struck the Indian Ocean nations on December 26, 2004, spread quickly around the globe. On every continent, nations and individuals were quick to promise and send aid of every kind — food, water, supplies for rebuilding, medicine, and in-kind donations. The generous outpouring speaks highly of the compassion people feel for the victims of one of nature's most dreadful displays of power.

However, now, several months after the disaster, much of the aid has not yet reached the people who so desperately need it. In some cases, lack of transportation and the remoteness of stricken villages are to blame. But some of the aid is tied up in committee, in meeting after meeting to decide who gets the aid, how much they get, and when. Other aid has not reached people because of arguments between factions of governments or tribes.

You may be one of those who, upon hearing of the disaster, sat right down to write a check for aid. If you are, it's time to write a letter to follow up that check. Write to the charitable group that you supported financially, following up on the money. Find out how far the aid has gotten, and ask for details about when more aid will reach the people who need it. Write your congressional representatives, too, and ask them to work with the governments of tsunami-ravaged nations, urging them to lay aside political differences for the good of their people.

So many have been helped — now let's make sure that ALL of the aid reaches ALL those who need it!

Claire Pennington
Des Moines, Iowa

On the Surface

1 Where are the people who need aid? _____

_____

2 Why do these people need aid? _____

_____

3 When did the destruction occur? _____

_____

4 What kinds of aid do the people need? _____

_____

5 How did people respond to the crisis? _____

_____

Discoveries

1 Write the meanings of the following words and phrases.

   a in-kind donations _____

   b compassion _____

   c remoteness _____

2 What is the usual way to address a letter to the editor? _____

_____

3 How might people close a letter to the editor? _____

_____

_____

Delving More Deeply

1 Why have people donated money and goods to the tsunami victims? _____

_____

_____

Reading Comprehension Across the Genres 7, SV 1419023624

2 What is the writer trying to persuade readers to do? _____

_____

3 What is keeping some aid from reaching some people? _____

_____

4 What does the writer think of how people around the world responded to the disaster?

_____

Hidden Depths

1 Many people donated money to express their grief and sympathy for the tsunami victims. Can you think of any other ways to express grief?

_____

_____

_____

2 Do you believe that richer countries should help countries in need? Explain why or why not.

_____

_____

_____

Extend Yourself

- Research the current rebuilding situation in the Indian Ocean nations struck by the tsunami. Use newspapers and the Internet to gather information; then update your classmates.
- Find out how tsunamis occur and whether they are likely to be a threat to either of our nation's coasts.
- On a map of the world, mark the nations affected by the tsunami.
- Write your own "letter to the editor" outlining your opinion on this matter.

 **LESSON 5** # "Private" to "Prize"

Cross-Curriculum Literacy Links: Science; History; Geography; Arts

Text Type	Dictionary
Purpose	To give the meaning, pronunciation, grammatical use, and history of words in a language
Structure	1 Head word
	2 Syllabification and Pronunciation
	3 Part of speech
	4 Definitions
	5 Phrases these words are used in
	6 Derivations
	7 Cross-references
	8 Etymology (origin)
Features	Abbreviations, font changes

From The American Heritage Dictionary of the English Language

privacy

privacy pri·va·cy /prī'və-sē/ — n. **1a.** The quality or condition of being secluded from the presence or view of others. **b.** The state of being free from unsanctioned intrusion: *a person's right to privacy.* **2.** The state of being concealed; secrecy.

private pri·vate /prī' vĭt/ — adj. **1a.** Secluded from the sight, presence, or intrusion of others: *a private hideaway.* **b.** Designed or intended for one's exclusive use: *a private room.* **2a.** Of or confined to the individual; personal: *a private joke; private opinions.* **b.** Undertaken on an individual basis: *private studies; private research.* **c.** Of, relating to, or receiving special hospital services and privileges: *a private patient.* **3.** Not available for public use, control, or participation: *a private club; a private party.* **4a.** Belonging to a particular person or persons, as opposed to the public or the government: *private property.* **b.** Of, relating to, or derived from nongovernment sources: *private funding.* **5.** Not holding an official or public position: *a private citizen.* **6a.** Not for

prize¹

public knowledge or disclosure; secret: *private papers; a private communication.* **b.** Not appropriate for use or display in public; intimate: *private behavior; a private tragedy.* **c.** Placing a high value on personal privacy: *a private person.* n. **1a.** abbr. **PVT** or **Pvt** or **Pvt.** A noncommissioned rank in the U.S. Army or Marine Corps that is below private first class. **b.** One who holds this rank or a similar rank in a military organization. **2. privates** Private parts. Often used with *the.*

privatize pri·va·tize /prī'və-tīz/ — v. To change (an industry or business, for example) from governmental or public ownership or control to private enterprise.

privatization pri'va·ti·za'tion (-tĭ-zā'shən) —NOUN

privet priv·et /prĭv'ĭt/ — n. **1.** Any of several shrubs of the genus *Ligustrum*, especially *L. vulgare* or *L. ovalifolium*, having opposite leaves and clusters of white flowers and widely used for hedges. **2.** Any of several similar or related plants. [origin unknown]

privilege priv·i·lege /prĭv′ə-lĭj, prĭv′lĭj/ — n. **1a.** A special advantage, immunity, permission, right, or benefit granted to or enjoyed by an individual, class, or caste. See synonyms at **right**. **b.** Such an advantage, immunity, or right held as a prerogative of status or rank, and exercised to the exclusion or detriment of others. **2.** The principle of granting and maintaining a special right or immunity: *a society based on privilege.* **3.** *Law* The right to privileged communication in a confidential relationship, as between client and attorney, patient and physician, or communicant and priest. **4.** An option to buy or sell a stock, including put, call, spread, and straddle.

privy priv·y / prĭv′ē/ — adj. **1.** Made a participant in knowledge of something private or secret: *was privy to classified information.*

2. Belonging or proper to a person, such as the British sovereign, in a private rather than official capacity. **3.** Secret; concealed. — n. (pl. **–ies**) **1a.** An outdoor toilet; an outhouse. **b.** A toilet. **2.** *Law* One of the parties having an interest in the same matter. Middle English *prive,* from Old French, from Latin *prīvātus,* private, from *prīvus,* single, alone.

prize¹ /prīz/ — n. **1.** Something offered or won as an award for superiority or victory, as in a contest or competition. **2.** Something worth striving for; a highly desirable possession. *adj.* **1.** Offered or given as a prize: *a prize cup.* **2.** Given a prize, or likely to win a prize: *a prize cow.* **3.** Worthy of a prize; first-class: *our prize azaleas.*

from *The American Heritage® Dictionary of the English Language: Fourth Edition.* 2000.

On the Surface

1 How many numbered definitions are there for the adjective *private?* _____

_____

2 How many numbered definitions are there for the noun *private?* _____

_____

3 What is written on the top left-hand side of the page? _____

_____

4 What is written on the top right-hand side of the page? _____

_____

Discoveries

1 Choose three words or phrases from the page and place them in a sentence that makes their meaning clear.

_____

_____

_____

2 Which word has the most definitions? _____

_____

Delving More Deeply

1 What are privies? _____

_____

2 List the jobs where people have privileged communication. _____

_____

3 Which word is used to describe when a business is transferred (sold) from government ownership to private ownership?

_____

4 Find the word that describes both the state of being undisturbed and the right to be undisturbed.

_____

Hidden Depths

1 Make a list of government-owned agencies you know of. _____

_____

_____

2 Write about what privacy means to you. _____

_____

_____

_____

_____

Extend Yourself

- Locate the dictionaries section in the library and list the different dictionaries you find there.
- Discuss with classmates how knowing a word's etymology can be useful.

LESSON (6) A Dog's Life

Cross-Curriculum Links: Arts

Text Type	Script
Purpose	To entertain, to make a social comment
Structure	1 Introduction — who or what, where and when
	2 Complication
	3 Series of events
	4 Resolution
Features	Character name, direct speech, stage directions

Characters: Frankie, a black lab; Muffin, a ginger cat; Slinky, a tabby cat; their owner, Jimmy

[at home on a sunny Saturday afternoon]

Muffin: [gets up, stretches] Hey, Slinky, wake up. They're back.

Slinky: [annoyed, turns his back toward Muffin] How many times have I told you that the name is Silver, not Slinky?

Muffin: That's not what Jimmy calls you. And besides, they're home, so get up. We've got work to do.

[Jimmy and Frankie enter.]

Jimmy: Hang on, boy — lemme get this leash off of you! [cats rub around his legs] Hello, cats — hungry, as usual? I'll get your food. [He goes into the kitchen.]

Muffin: Works every time!

Slinky: It's a living. Barely.

Frankie: Guys! Guys! You should've gone with us. I keep tellin' ya! It's so much fun! [He chases his tail a minute, then settles down on the rug.]

Slinky: [with interruptions for grooming] Ridiculous creature. Why he wants to get in that car is more than I can comprehend.

Frankie: Oh, come on — the wind in your face, the feel of the road zipping by under you—all the things you see — you gotta admit that it's pretty cool!

Muffin: It does sound . . . interesting. We never see anything but the house and what's just outside the windows.

Slinky: Please. Wind in my face? Do you have any idea how much time I've put in on these whiskers? [He strokes them with a paw.] Besides, when we're in the car, all we see is the inside of the crate. And I'm fortunate if Mr. Claustrophobia here doesn't throw up on me.

Frankie: But then you get to the park, and you play catch, and you see other dogs and kids, and you can run and run, as long as you come back when Jimmy whistles.

Slinky: Oh, joy. Dirt and sweat and children pawing your fur, just when you've got it groomed well. I tell you what: You can keep your park. I don't want to go any further than the kitchen to eat my kibble. [stalks off]

Muffin: Next time, Frankie, help me stow away.

Frankie: Sure thing, pal! Only — promise you won't throw up on me?

On the Surface

1   What is unusual about the characters in this dramatic excerpt? _____

_____

2   Name the characters and explain how they are related. _____

_____

_____

3   What work do the cats have to do when Jimmy comes home? _____

_____

4   Where have Frankie and Jimmy been? _____

_____

5   Are the animals male characters or female characters? How can you tell? _____

_____

_____

Discoveries

1   Write the meanings of the following words.

   a   ginger   _____

   b   ridiculous   _____

   c   comprehend   _____

   d   claustrophobia   _____

   e   kibble   _____

2   Rank the animal characters in terms of their speech, from least formal to most formal.

_____

Delving More Deeply

1   What does Slinky's comment about his name tell you about his character?

_____

_____

Reading Comprehension Across the Genres 7, SV 1419023624

2 In what important way do Muffin and Slinky respond differently to Frankie's description of the outside world?

_____

_____

_____

3 Whose lines have the most exclamation points? Why do you think this is?

_____

_____

4 What is Slinky's main objection to going outside? _____

_____

_____

Hidden Depths

1 What stereotypes of cat and dog behavior can you think of? Does the excerpt question those stereotypes?

_____

_____

_____

2 Several live-action movies have been made recently in which dogs, cats, and other animals have major speaking roles. List two or three of these movies. Why do you think screenwriters and directors put the thoughts, words, and actions of people into animals' roles?

_____

_____

_____

Extend Yourself

• What is a beast fable? Find out; then read several beast fables. Choose one to act out for the class, converting the fable to a script and performing it with classmates.

• Write the next scene of this drama, in which Muffin stows away and heads out for a great adventure. Submit your scene to your classmates for consideration.

• What animated children's movies featuring animals, such as Disney's *Bambi*, did you enjoy while young? Choose one to view again, and write a review of it from your now more mature perspective. Does it still have something to teach you?

LESSON 7 In the Science Lab

Cross-Curriculum Literacy Links: Science

Text Type	Procedure/Instructions
Purpose	To give instructions or show how something is accomplished through a series of steps
Structure	1 Opening statement of goal or aim
	2 Material required named in order of use
	3 Series of steps listed in chronological order
Features	Logical sequence of steps; may use technical language and diagrams

Experiment 6.1 Sources of Heat

How can we obtain heat?

In most cases, you can tell if heat is being produced by slowly bringing the back of your hand towards the likely source of heat.

1 Friction
   Rub your hands together; rub two pieces of wood together; saw a piece of wood; file some metal.

2 Chemical
   a Light a candle; light some methylated spirits in a dish; light a Bunsen burner.
   b Add some dilute hydrochloric acid to dilute caustic soda (sodium hydroxide).

3 Electrical
   Plug in and turn on a radiator; connect some resistance wire to a battery; connect a lamp to a battery.

4 Sun
   Use a magnifying glass to focus some light from the sun on either some paper or onto a dead leaf.

DO NOT FOCUS THE LIGHT ONTO YOUR BODY
DO NOT LOOK AT THE SUN THROUGH A MAGNIFYING GLASS

from *The World of Science: Book 2*, Second ed. Eds. David A. Heffernan and Mark S. Learmonth. Melbourne: Longman Cheshire, 1989. P. 122.

On the Surface

1 There are four main sources of heat used in this procedure. List them. _____

_____

2 List the materials needed to produce heat chemically. _____

_____

_____

3 When using a magnifying glass, what should you not do? _____

_____

4 How can you tell if heat is being produced? _____

_____

5 What is the other name for caustic soda? _____

_____

Discoveries

1 What does the title of this piece ("experiment") mean? _____

_____

2 How does knowing this definition affect how you read the text? _____

_____

_____

3 List three features that indicate that this text consists of instructions or a procedure.

_____

_____

_____

Delving More Deeply

1 List the sources of heat that can also produce fire.

_____

_____

2 Which source of heat involves heat being produced through movement?

_____

3 Which source of heat is produced by connecting to a source of energy?

_____

4 Sources of heat need a source of energy. List the source of energy for the heat sources in this experiment.

_____

_____

Hidden Depths

1 Which sources of heat do you use most often and for what purpose? _____

_____

_____

_____

2 If the sources of heat you used most often were not available to you, which other sources would you use?

_____

_____

_____

Extend Yourself

- With the help of your science teacher, complete the experiments and write a report.
- Research alternative energy sources and complete a poster about them.
- Select one of the experiments and present a demonstration to the class, explaining how to perform the experiment.

LESSON 8 Light and Mirrors

Cross-Curriculum Literacy Links: Science

Text Type	Explanation
Purpose	To inform, to explain how or why things are as they are or how things work
Structure	**1** A general statement
	2 Series of statement or events in chronological or logical order
	3 Concluding statement
Features	Logical sequence of details or ideas; may use headings, diagrams, and tables

Mirror, Mirror on the Wall

"Mirror, mirror on the wall, who's the fairest of them all?" From ancient times, reflections from pools of water, polished stones and metallic objects were thought to be magical. Today, mirrors are used for many different purposes. We use them every day to see our reflection and to see behind us and around corners when we are cycling or driving, for example.

Light

To understand how mirrors produce images, we need to understand what light does, because it is light that brings images to our eyes. This light comes from many sources, such as the sun, light bulbs and flashlights.

One of the most important properties of light is that it travels in straight lines. It leaves its source and travels in a straight line until it reaches another surface or the eye of the observer. You may have noticed that it does this if you shine a flashlight in a dark room.

Making a Shadow

If there is something blocking the path of the light that the light cannot pass through, then it cannot reach the observer and a shadow is created. If light did not travel in straight lines there would be no such things as shadows.

Reflection

Another important thing that light does is that when it hits the surface of something, some or all of it bounces back, like a ball bouncing off a wall. Like the bouncing ball, as it travels back away from the surface it again moves in a straight line. We call this bouncing back reflection, and if it wasn't for this ability to reflect we could not see ourselves in a mirror.

from *Nelson Junior Science Series* by Rachael Whittle. Unpublished.

On the Surface

1 From what did people long ago see reflections? _____

_____

2 Give two examples of what we use mirrors for today. _____

_____

_____

3 What is one of the most important properties of light? _____

4 How can you test whether light travels in a straight line? _____

_____

5 What can change the direction light travels in? _____

_____

Discoveries

1 Look up these words in a dictionary and write your own meanings for them.

   a fairest _____

   b reflection _____

   c polished _____

   d metallic _____

   e magical _____

   f images _____

   g properties _____

   h source _____

   i ability _____

2 What does light do when it hits a surface? _____

_____

Delving More Deeply

1 How are shadows formed? _____

_____

_____

2 What does the fact that we can see ourselves in a mirror prove? _____

_____

3 Which of the following statements is true? Circle the correct answer.

   a Light keeps going in the same line forever.

   b If light did not go in straight lines, we would not see our image in a mirror.

   c When light hits surfaces, all of it always bounces back.

   d Only mirrors can produce reflections.

4 How does the existence of shadows prove that light travels in straight lines?

_____

_____

5 If light could pass through everything, would you ever see shadows?

_____

Hidden Depths

1 Why do you think people in ancient times thought reflections were magical?

_____

_____

2 Make a list of the everyday uses you have for mirrors.

_____

_____

_____

Extend Yourself

• Conduct some experiments using a flashlight, a mirror, a light, and a darkened room. Write a brief report on your findings.

• List all the stories you know of that feature mirrors or reflections with magical qualities, e.g., Snow White, Harry Potter, Narcissus. Explain what the characters see in the mirror or reflection that is so important.

• Whenever people look in a mirror, they not only see what they look like, but they are also aware that the reflection shows what other people see. Try putting on your grumpiest face while looking at yourself in the mirror. Now try your happiest face. Write an account of how different you looked.

LESSON ⑨ Out in Space

Cross-Curriculum Literacy Links: Science; Geography

Text Type Narrative — science fiction
Purpose To tell a story; includes a basis of scientific fact or theory
Structure 1 Introduction — who or what, where and when (fantasy world)
2 Complication, damaged world/environment
3 Series of events to save the world/survive
4 Resolution
Features Use of past tense, pronouns, technical or scientific language

From Rocket Ship Galileo

"Goshawmighty," exclaimed Art, "this is something!"

He unlimbered his equipment and began snapping frantically, until Ross pointed out that his lens cover was still on. Then he steadied down. Ross floated face down and stared out at the desolation. They were speeding silently along, only two hundred miles above the ground, and they were approaching the sunrise line of light and darkness. The shadows were long on the barren wastes below them, the mountain peaks and the great gaping craters more horrendous on that account. "It's scary," Ross decided. "I'm not sure I like it."

"Want off at the next corner?" Cargraves inquired.

"No, but I'm not dead certain I'm glad I came."

Morrie grasped his arm, to steady himself apparently, but quite as much for the comfort of solid human companionship. "You know what I think, Ross," he began, as he stared out at the endless miles of craters. "I think I know how it got that way. Those aren't volcanic craters, that's certain — and it wasn't done by meteors. They did it themselves!"

"Huh? Who?"

"The moon people. They did it. They wrecked themselves. They ruined themselves. They had one atomic war too many."

"Huh? What the —" Ross stared, then looked back at the surface as if to read the grim mystery there.

Art stopped taking pictures.

"How about it, Doc?"

Cargraves wrinkled his brow. "Could be," he admitted. "None of the other theories for natural causes hold water for one reason or another. It would account for the relatively smooth parts we call 'seas.'"

"They really were seas; that's why they weren't hit very hard."

"And that's why they aren't seas any more," Morrie went on. "They blew their atmosphere off and the seas boiled away. Look at Tycho. That's where they set off the biggest ammunition dump on the planet. I'll bet somebody worked out a counter-weapon that worked too well. It set off every atom bomb on the moon all at once and it ruined them! I'm sure of it."

"Well," said Cargraves, "I'm not sure of it, but I admit the theory is attractive. Perhaps we'll find out when we land."

from "Rocket Ship Galileo" by Robert A. Heinlein, in *Classic Science Fiction*, Ed. Peter Haining. Sutton: Macmillan, 1998. Pp. 8–9.

On the Surface

1 What is the name of the rocket ship? _____

_____

2 What are the explorers floating 200 miles above? _____

_____

3 What do they see? _____

_____

4 List the people who are on the ship. _____

_____

5 What is Morrie's theory as to how the craters got there? _____

_____

Discoveries

1 Write the meanings of the following words.

  a desolation _____

  b barren _____

  c horrendous _____

  d meteors _____

2 Find a picture or draw a scene which shows desolation.

3 What does the phrase "doesn't hold water" mean? _____

_____

Delving More Deeply

1   According to the story, which place has the biggest ammunition dump on the planet?

_____

2   What evidence supports their theory that the moon people ruined themselves? Circle the correct answer.

   a   They had one atomic war too many.

   b   The desolation

   c   The relatively smooth part called the seas

3   Explain what happened to the seas. _____

_____

4   What do you think Cargraves needs to do before he will be sure of Morrie's theory?

_____

Hidden Depths

1   What do you think has happened to the moon people? _____

_____

_____

_____

2   How do the men feel about landing on the moon? What do you think they will find there?

_____

_____

_____

Extend Yourself

•   Find out about the effects of atomic/nuclear bombs, particularly at Hiroshima and Nagasaki.

•   Do research to learn about positive uses of nuclear energy. Design a bulletin board with your classmates to teach other students about the advantages — and the challenges — of nuclear energy uses.

 **LESSON 10 It's a "Bad" Thing**

Cross-Curriculum Literacy Links: Science; History; Civics and Citizenship

---

Text Type Thesaurus
Purpose To aid the expression of ideas in writing, to increase vocabulary
Structure 1 Alphabetical
2 Slang and informal words included
Features Abbreviations, font changes

From The Oxford Australian Student's Thesaurus

bad adj. **1.** *Bad person or deed.* abhorrent, abominable, atrocious, awful, base, beastly, corrupt, despicable, detestable, dishonest, evil, hateful, immoral, infamous, loathsome, malevolent, malicious, mean, naughty, notorious, sinful, undesirable, ungodly, unkind, unrighteous, unworthy, vile, villainous, wicked. SEE ALSO **cruel.** OPP. good. **2.** *bad weather.* appalling (inf.), atrocious (inf.), foul, lousy (sl.), shocking (inf.), terrible, unpleasant. OPP. fair, fine. **3.** *bad conditions.* abysmal, adverse, appalling (inf.), deplorable, hopeless, pitiful, unfavourable, unpleasant, woeful. **4.** *It was a bad accident.* appalling, awful, dire, disastrous, dreadful, frightful, ghastly, hideous, horrible, horrific, horrifying, nasty, serious, severe, shocking, terrible. OPP. minor, slight. **5.** *The food had been left out of the refrigerator and was all bad.* decayed, foul, mildewed, mouldy, off, putrid, rotten, spoiled, tainted. OPP. fresh. **6.** *a bad smell.* foul, offensive, on the nose (Austral. sl.), revolting, stinking, vile. OPP. fragrant, pleasant. **7.** *bad workmanship.* defective, faulty, incompetent, inferior, poor, shoddy, unsatisfactory, unsound, worthless. OPP. good. **8.** *a bad business.* **9.** *She always feels bad.* crook (Austral. & NZ sl.), ill, off color, poorly, sick, unhealthy, unwell. OPP. fine. **10.** *Sweets are bad for your teeth.* damaging, deleterious, destructive, harmful, hurtful, ruinous, undesirable, unhealthy. OPP. good. **bad blood** enmity. **bad language** abuse, expletives, invective, obscenities, swearwords, vituperation. **bad-tempered** adj. angry, crook (Austral. & NZ sl.), cross, hot-tempered, ill-tempered, maggoty (Austral. sl.)

from *The Oxford Australian Student's Thesaurus.* Melbourne: Oxford University Press, 1991. P. 29.

On the Surface

1   The topics for the adjective *bad* are numbered and written in italics. Write out the topics.

_____

_____

2 Adjectives are defining words. The adjectives for *bad person* are listed

    a in order of importance.

    b in order of relevance.

    c alphabetically.

3 What are the opposite words for *bad accident?* _____

_____

4 What is the "SEE ALSO" word given for *bad person or deed?* _____

_____

5 Slang is highly informal (colloquial) language. Often slang conveys negative associations. List two slang words used to describe bad weather.

_____

Discoveries

1 Look up *bad* in the dictionary. Write out the definition. How is the definition similar to or different from the entry in the thesaurus?

_____

2 Circle eight words that are used to describe a bad person or a bad deed. (They can be vertical, horizontal, diagonal, or back-to-front.)

```
T N E L O V E L A M A
Y A L U F E T A H B B
L U N G O D L Y H A O
T G O E S O B O S B M
S H L G L S R E I S I
A T U U I R R F G M N
E Y F O E N A E M E A
B W U N W O R N I L B
A G T M O S H T A I L
B D E K C I W L I V E
Q B I S L U F N I S T
```

Delving More Deeply

1   List behavior which could be described as "base." (See the first definition.)

_____

2   Write a short paragraph, using some of the words listed in topics 2, 3 and 4, to describe bad weather and bad driving conditions that result in a bad accident.

_____

_____

3   Find two words in the list that describe a person who has a reputation for bad behavior.

_____

4   Make a list of words which describe mildly bad behavior and those which are high-level bad behavior.

_____

_____

Hidden Depths

1   Describe an experience when you have behaved badly, or you have witnessed someone behaving badly. Outline what happened and use one of the adjectives listed to describe the behavior.

_____

_____

_____

2   Discuss in small groups a notorious/infamous person. What did he or she do? Which words could you use to describe the behavior of this person?

_____

_____

_____

Extend Yourself

•   What are the latest slang uses of the word *bad?* Write a short conversation in which the speakers use the word. Perform the conversation with a classmate.

•   Create a word web or other graphic organizer to show how the various meanings of *bad* are related to each other. Display your web for classmates.

LESSON 11 # Which Book?

Cross-Curriculum Literacy Links: Arts

Text Type   Book review
Purpose   To give details and opinion on a text
Structure   Review
    1 Context — background information on the text, details about author (other texts, prizes, etc.)
    2 Description of the text (including characters and plot)
    3 Intended audience
    4 Concluding statement (judgment, opinion, or recommendation)
Features   Language may be formal or informal depending on purpose and audience; may include examples and quotes, publisher and price

The Age Summer Book Guide

ROVER SAVES CHRISTMAS

Roddy Doyle SCHOLASTIC PRESS $24.95 HC

You don't remember Rover? Well, you ought to. The hero of last year's adventure, *The Giggler Treatment*, Rover is a rather amazing dog. He can travel at supersonic speed, and has made a fortune exploiting his talents. It's Christmas Eve in Dublin and disaster is looming. Jimmy and Robby Mack are so desperate for Santa's arrival that they've made twenty-seven sandwiches for Santa and peeled carrots for Rudolph. But there's a big problem. Rudolph is off sick and the sleigh is grounded. Can Rover save the day for Jimmy, Robby and millions of other boys and girls? Roddy Doyle, author of the Booker Prize-winning *Paddy Clarke Ha, Ha, Ha* shows his remarkable ability to write rude and hilarious kids' books.

THE HOSTILE HOSPITAL: A SERIES OF UNFORTUNATE EVENTS, BOOK THE EIGHTH

Lemony Snicket HARPERCOLLINS $17.95 HC

Those poor, pathetic Baudelaire Orphans! Just when you think things couldn't get any worse for them, our narrator finds more hard times for Violet, Klaus and Sunny. According to Lemony Snicket, "This book . . . describes every last detail of the Baudelaire children's miserable stay at Heimlich Hospital, which makes it one of the most dreadful books in the world. There are many pleasant things to read about, but this book contains none of them." Now clearly this makes the reviewer's task that much more difficult. Imagine trying to say something nice about the awful lives of these nice children? Perhaps you'd like to try yourselves?

Also available: *The Bad Beginning* (1), *The Reptile Room* (2), *The Wide Window* (3), *The Miserable Mill* (4), *The Austere Academy* (5), *The Ersatz Elevator* (6) *The Vile Village* (7).

COUNTING CROCODILES

Judy Sierra Illustrated by Will Hillenbrand VOYAGER $16.75 PB

"The Sillabobble crocodiles thought they were truly cool, and they looked upon those waters as their private swimming pool. They appeared to be quite vicious, feasting fearlessly on fishes." Poor monkey. All she has to eat are sour lemons. One day she spies a banana tree on a faraway island, but the only way to get there is to navigate the crocodile-infested waters of the Sillabobble Sea. That's no problem when you're a brave, clever monkey who knows how to count to ten and back. Bright, full color, very funny illustrations to complement the text make this a must for the pre-school set.

"The Age Summer Book Guide," from *The Age*. Melbourne, November 2001.

On the Surface

1   Fill in the table with details of the books reviewed.

Author	Title	Publisher	Price

2   Name the title of the previous year's Rover book by Roddy Doyle. _____

_____

3   List the titles of the seven other books in *A Series of Unfortunate Events* by Lemony Snicket.

_____

_____

_____

4   Who is the intended audience for "Counting Crocodiles"? _____

_____

Discoveries

1   Write the meanings of the following words.

   a exploiting _____

   b looming _____

   c hilarious _____

   d pathetic _____

   e miserable _____

2   Alliteration is the repetition of the same sound at the beginning of words, usually appearing in the same sentence, e.g., "President promotes party." Find an example in the reviews.

_____

3   Make a list of the words you think try to persuade you to buy one of the books.

_____

40

Delving More Deeply

1 Which age group do you think "Counting Crocodiles" is appropriate for? Explain why.

_____

2 What is the reviewer's opinion of "Counting Crocodiles"? Write a quote of the reviewer's opinion.

_____

3 What is the story line for *Rover Saves Christmas?* _____

_____

_____

4 Who do you think the intended audience is for these reviews? _____

_____

Hidden Depths

1 Which book would you like to read? Explain what in particular appeals to you. If you do not like the sound of these books, explain why not.

_____

_____

2 Would you read a review such as this if you were looking to read or purchase a book for yourself or for a gift? Explain how it would be useful.

_____

_____

3 Where else could you find information on texts? _____

_____

Extend Yourself

• Survey your classmates: What are their favorite books? Ask each student to explain why he or she liked the book.

• Do a Web search to find the biography of an author.

• Create an advertising poster either for books you have read or for your favorite author.

LESSON 12 · At the Truck Stop

Cross-Curriculum Literacy Links: Difference and Diversity

Text Type	Description
Purpose	To describe the characteristic features of a particular thing
Structure	1 Opening statement — introduction to the subject
	2 Characteristic features of the subject
	3 Concluding comment (optional)
Features	Details involving senses to assist readers to visualize a scene or event

From A Bridge to Wiseman's Cove

Prelude

The lights of the service station created a circle of warmth and movement amid the darkness. Weary travelers pulled in from the highway, gathering like moths around a grimy bulb to refill the petrol tank, stretch aching muscles and hunch over a cup of tea for a few minutes in the all-night café. None of these travelers noticed a lonely figure who shunned the bright light to wait among the semitrailers parked at the edge of the tarmac. Only when a bus halted nearby, its air brakes hissing, the gravel crushed and crackling under the massive wheels, did the figure stir and creep to the corner of an enormous prime mover to watch as the passengers stepped down and wandered, yawning, into the café.

An elderly man was the last to leave. He lowered an arthritic leg gingerly from the bottom step, leaning heavily on the driver who waited patiently below. With this man safely on solid ground, the driver closed the door and headed off towards the lights in the wake of his passengers. The figure stepped from the darkness and tried the door. Locked.

Twenty minutes later the driver returned, leading this time an informal line of travelers at his back. With a quick twist of his key, the door folded open and he stood aside to let them pass. The stragglers would be a few moments yet so he climbed aboard, easing into the seat as they came in ones and twos. He didn't notice a woman step from the shadow of a removal van and close up behind a pair of sleepy teenagers. She mounted the steps, careful to keep the tell-tale knapsack concealed as best she could and continued down the bus, nonchalantly checking the webbed pockets behind each seat until she found an empty one. She slipped into the seat, then leaned forward, taking an age to tie and re-tie her shoelaces.

The front door sighed as it closed and the bus lurched forward, to pause briefly at the edge of the highway. A car swept past, leaving the road behind it suddenly black and empty. The driver gunned the engine, commanding its throaty roar and the bus pulled away from the road-house into the sea of darkness.

Only then did the woman sit up and permit herself a smile.

from *A Bridge to Wiseman's Cove* by James Moloney. Brisbane: University of Queensland Press, 1996. P. 1.

On the Surface

1 Where was the lonely figure waiting? _____

_____

2 Where did the driver go during the twenty-minute break? _____

_____

3 Who did the woman hide behind as she climbed in the bus? _____

_____

4 What was the woman careful to keep concealed? _____

_____

5 Why did the bus pause briefly at the edge of the tarmac? _____

_____

Discoveries

1 Write the meanings of the following words.

   a grimy   _____

   b hunch   _____

   c lonely   _____

   d shunned   _____

   e creep   _____

   f gingerly   _____

   g patiently   _____

   h nonchalantly   _____

2 From which point of view is the passage written: first person or third person?

_____

3 Is the passage written in the past or present tense? _____

_____

4 Similes are comparisons that use the words *like* or *as*, e.g., "It was light as day." Find an example of simile in the text.

_____

    Reading Comprehension Across the Genres 7, SV 1419023624

Delving More Deeply

1 How does the writer establish early in the passage that the woman is hiding?

_____

_____

2 Why does she check the web-pockets? _____

_____

3 What time of day do you think the passage is set in? Why? _____

_____

4 Make a list of words used in the passage to describe the woman's behavior. What impression do they give of her?

_____

_____

_____

Hidden Depths

1 Write your own description of the woman, or draw it. What does she look like, what is she wearing, and so on?

_____

_____

2 How effective is the passage in capturing your attention? Do you want to keep on reading? What do you want to know?

_____

_____

_____

Extend Yourself

- Descriptive writing should not only describe the setting and behavior of people in the text; it should also capture the mood or sense of what it was like to be in that place at that time. List the sounds described in the passage.

- The passage has many images (word pictures) that help us "see" the scene. List the images.

- Smell is not included. Describe the smells that would relate to this passage.

- Where is she going? Write your own story following on from this passage. Decide if you will continue in the third person. You may also slip into the first person, becoming the woman on the bus or someone else on the bus. Start with the next "scene." Remember to include sights and sounds, e.g., action: shrunk, curled, collapsed into the seat; face: smiled, frowned, wrinkled.

LESSON 13 Running Behind, Catching Up

Cross-Curriculum Literacy Link: Arts

Text Type	Rap poem
Purpose	To entertain and express feelings and ideas
Structure	Rhyming and rhythmic patterns, repetition of words or sounds
Features	Careful word choice for meaning and sound

Late Is a Way of Life

Alarm wrecks my dreams at seven-thirty
Late is a way of life for me
Look around for a shirt that's not too dirty
I said — Late is a way of life

Gulp down a smoothie, can't be late
Late is a way of life for me
Bus pulls away at ten till eight
I said — Late is a way of life

Gotta get to my desk by eight thirty-four
Late is a way of life for me
'Cause that's when the teacher shuts the door
I said — Late is a way of life

Late is a way of life
Uh-unh, no way
Late is a way of life
Think about it

Race through the lunch line, it'll be closed soon
Late is a way of life for me
Just markin' time till the afternoon
I said — Late is a way of life

Finally make it home, now my day slows down
Late is a way of life for me
The clock hands start to drag around
I said — Late is a way of life

Nowhere to go and nothing to do
Late is a way of life for me
Now the time doesn't matter and I'm breezin'
     through
I said — Late is a way of life

Late is a way of life
Uh-unh, no way
Late is a way of life
Think about it

On the Surface

1   Who is the speaker?

_____

2   What is the first thing the teen does when he or she wakes up?

_____

3   Why is he or she in such a hurry?

_____

Reading Comprehension Across the Genres 7, SV 1419023624

4 How does the speaker explain his or her tardiness? _____

_____

5 Why is lateness not an issue in the afternoon? _____

_____

Discoveries

1 Write the meanings of the following words.

a smoothie _____

b breezin' _____

2 How do the stresses — the beats — fall in the first line of the poem? Write the stressed syllables in capital letters and the unstressed syllables in lowercase letters. Does this rhythm carry on through the poem?

_____

_____

_____

Delving More Deeply

1 What comment does the refrain (stanzas 4 and 8) make about the speaker's lateness?

_____

_____

2 List examples of word choice that create the poem's informal tone. _____

_____

3 Why hasn't the writer used periods, commas, question marks, or exclamation points?

_____

_____

_____

_____

4 What ideas and words are repeated? What is the effect of this repetition?

_____

_____

_____

_____

Hidden Depths

1   Are you usually early, on time, or running behind? What does this habit say about your personality and organizational skills?

_____

_____

_____

2   Why are the second and fourth lines of each stanza italicized? _____

_____

_____

_____

Extend Yourself

• Use the Internet to research ways to overcome counter-productive habits such as lateness. Develop a method to overcome bad habits and share it with your classmates.

• Use the Internet to find out about a new invention from the tech lab at the Massachusetts Institute of Technology (MIT): an alarm clock that rolls away after the user hits the snooze button. Report your findings to the class.

• Write your own rap poem about a habit that's a way of life for you. Comment on the habit's helpfulness or hindrance in the poem.

LESSON 14 Knights on Horseback

Cross-Curriculum Literacy Links: History

Text Type   Historical report
Purpose   To reconstruct past experiences by telling events in the order in which they occurred
Structure   1 Introduction — background information about who, where, and when
                2 Series of events in chronological order
                3 A personal comment
Features   Use of past tense, action verbs, descriptive language; may include quotes

Becoming a Knight

Knights had a high position in medieval society. Because conditions were often violent and unsettled, military power was very important. The knights were a warrior elite, and their status in society reflected this importance.

A Warrior Elite

Knights fought on horseback as cavalry troops. The cavalry were the most important troops in medieval armies. Their armor, equipment and war-horses were very expensive, and few people could afford them. At great fairs in Champagne in the thirteenth century, for example, war-horses were sold for about £85 each. It would take an ordinary foot-soldier 32 years to earn that amount of money.

Becoming a Knight

The sons of knights were sent to the household of another knight at about the age of twelve to learn the skills of knighthood. They were trained by serving the knight in many ways — by grooming his horses and looking after his armor, for example. A young man who served a knight in this way was called a "squire." Squires also learned to ride and fight on horseback, and to look after weapons. One skill considered particularly important was how to serve the lord with food at table.

By the thirteenth century complicated ceremonies had developed to mark the occasion on which a man finally became a knight. On the day before the ceremony, the knight-to-be took a special bath, and then dressed in white clothes. He spent the night in prayer in church, kneeling in front of the altar on which his sword and armor lay. Early the next morning mass was said in church, then the knight was dressed in his armor. Prayers were said over the armor and sword. These were intended to dedicate the knight and his work to God. Finally another knight dealt him a blow on the neck with his hand or sword. The new knight vowed to act according to the code of chivalry.

from *The World of the Medieval Knight* by Christopher Gravett. London: Hodder Children's Books, 1993. P. 20.

On the Surface

1   What position did knights have in medieval society? _____

2   Which were the most important troops in medieval armies? _____

3   What could few people afford to buy? _____

4   Who would be sent to the household of a knight to learn the skills of knighthood?

_____

5   List the duties a squire (knight in training) would be expected to learn.

_____

Discoveries

1   Find out the meaning of *chivalry* and write your own definition. _____

_____

_____

2   Define *elite*. Who do you believe are the elite of our society today? _____

_____

_____

Delving More Deeply

1   Fill in a daily schedule below for a squire.

5:00–6:30 A.M. _____

7:00–9:00 A.M. _____

9:30 A.M.–12:00 NOON _____

1:00–4:30 P.M. _____

6:00–8:00 P.M. _____

2   Devise a chart that outlines in detail the two-day procedure for becoming a knight.

Day before	Day of ceremony

Reading Comprehension Across the Genres 7, SV 1419023624

3 To whom does the knight dedicate himself in the ceremony? _____

4 Why did knights have such a high position in medieval society? _____

_____

Hidden Depths

1 You are a twelve-year-old squire who has just started his training. Write a letter home. Share and discuss.

2 Who are the "warrior elite" in today's military? Outline the skills these people would need to have. Include personal qualities a soldier needs to have.

_____

_____

_____

Extend Yourself

- Make your own coat of arms. Include four symbols that tell something about your family, background, environment, and personal interests.

- Research famous knights. Write a report on your findings.

- View some of the latest films about knights and write a review. Or view some old classics.

- Write an advertisement for a new squire. List the qualities that you require. Alternatively, write an advertisement for a "Knight in Shining Armor."

- Read novels about knights and life in medieval times.

More advanced readers might try:

  — *Mammoth Book of Arthurian Legends* edited by Mike Ashley

  — *The Winter King* by Bernard Cornwell

  — *The Mists of Avalon* by Marion Zimmer Bradley

  — Poetry: Tennyson's "Morte d'Arthur."

Write a book report and present it to your class.

- Devise an obstacle course for knights in training.

NAME _____   DATE _____

LESSON 15 · Sailing the World

Cross-Curriculum Literacy Links: Geography; Science; Civics and Citizenship

Text Type	Map
Purpose	To show locations and features
Structure	Pictorial representation of a region
Features	Visual information; combining words, symbols and images

Jesse's Voyage

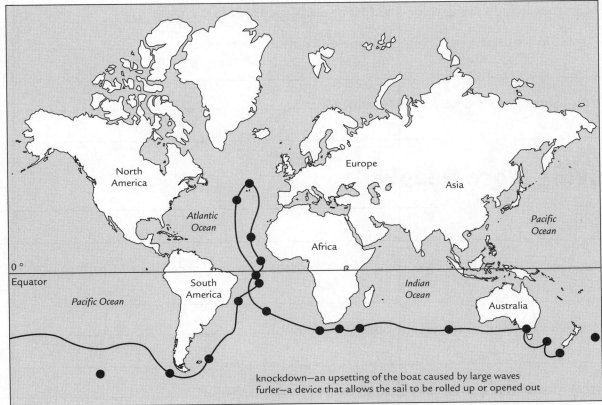

knockdown—an upsetting of the boat caused by large waves
furler—a device that allows the sail to be rolled up or opened out

1 departed 7 December 1998,
   arrived 31 October 1999
2 Christmas Day
3 met fishermen
4 first bad weather

5 position of rescued Autissier
6 first proper knockdown
7 second knockdown
8 whale encounter
9 becalmed for four days

10 close call with tanker
11 met family
12 pirate scare
13 furler problem
14 passed over previous track

15 third knockdown
16 force 10 storm
17 no power
18 eighteenth birthday
19 mid Indian rough patch

redrawn from *Lionheart: A Journey of the Human Spirit*, by Jesse Martin (with Ed Gannon),
Sydney: Allen & Unwin, 2000. Pp. viii–ix.

On the Surface

1 Whose journey does the map depict? _____

2 When did he depart? _____

3 Where did he depart from? _____

4 When did he arrive home? _____

5 How many times did Jesse cross the equator? _____

Discoveries

1 In which direction did Jesse sail? _____

2 In which hemisphere was Jesse for most of his journey? _____

3 Using an atlas, add the Cape of Good Hope and Cape Horn to the map.

4 Where did Jesse meet his family? Add these islands to the key. _____

_____

5 What happens when a sailboat is becalmed? _____

_____

Delving More Deeply

1 What does the key show? _____

_____

2 How many days did it take Jesse to sail from Australia to where he celebrated Christmas Day?

_____

3 In which ocean did Jesse have the fewest problems? _____

_____

4 Which part of the journey do you think was the most dangerous? _____

_____

5 Why do you think Jesse met up with his family where he did? _____

_____

52

Hidden Depths

1 How do you think Jesse spent his eighteenth birthday? Write his diary entry for this day.

_____

_____

_____

2 Write what you know about pirates. _____

_____

_____

_____

Extend Yourself

- Read Jesse's book. Write a brief summary of the nineteen events noted on the map. Write a report of what happened, where he was, and what he did.

- Undertake research about modern-day piracy. On a map, mark the areas where there are piracy problems. Write a report on what happens and how the authorities are attempting to deal with it.

- Research the naval history of ships passing the Cape of Good Hope and Cape Horn. Write a report on your findings.

- Get permission to view the film *White Squall* on video.

LESSON (16) Graphic Information

Cross-Curriculum Literacy Links: Geography; Science; Mathematics

Text Type	Pictograph
Purpose	Visual communication of information
Structure	1 Pictures/images/signs
	2 Symbols
	3 Illustrations
	4 Tables
Features	Statistical information presented as a graphic illustration; visually accurate relationship between the picture and figures presented

Transportation and the Atmosphere

	Number of passengers per automobile, bus, or train car	Number of miles per person per gallon of fuel
car		21.7
		88.9
bus		124.3
train		136.1

adapted from *The Acid Rain Hazard* by Judith Woodburn. Milwaukee: Gareth Stevens Publishing, 1992. P. 24.

Reading Comprehension Across the Genres 7, SV 1419023624

On the Surface

1   What are the three modes of transport shown in the chart? _____
_____

2   What do the two other columns in the graph show? _____
_____

_____

3   What is the title of the chart? _____
_____

4   Does the chart tell us anything about the atmosphere? _____
_____

5   How many passengers are accounted for on the bus? How many on the train?
_____

Discoveries

1   What does the word *per* mean? Find out its etymology. _____
_____

2   What terms do countries that use the metric system use for "gallon" and "mile" to measure amounts of fuel and distances?

_____

_____

Delving More Deeply

1   How many miles can one person travel per gallon of fuel when traveling by train?
_____

2   What is the graph implying about the effect of certain modes of transport on the atmosphere?

_____

_____

3   If traveling by car, what does the chart suggest you should do? _____
_____

4   Which mode of transport is the most environmentally friendly? _____

Hidden Depths

1 List any current government policies that encourage fuel efficiency. If you can't think of any, suggest some strategies to encourage people to be more fuel-efficient in regard to transportation.

_____

_____

_____

2 Which modes of transport do you mainly use? List the advantages/disadvantages of each.

_____

_____

_____

Extend Yourself

• Research and write a report about the effect of pollution on the atmosphere. Present this information as a chart/poster.

• Does your city have public transportation? Find a map of train and bus lines in your city. Plan a trip from home to school, the city, or a friend's place. How much would it cost? What do you need to know to get there?

• If your city does not have public transportation, write a letter to your city manager or council outlining the benefits to people and the environment of such a system.

• Make a poster encouraging people to use public transport or to carpool.

LESSON (17) Acid Rain

Cross-Curriculum Literacy Links: Geography; Science; Mathematics

Text Type	Explanation — geography
Purpose	To inform and explain how or why things are as they are or how things work
Structure	1 A general statement
	2 A series of statements in chronological or logical order
	3 Concluding statement
Features	Logical sequence of details or ideas; may use headings, diagrams and tables

Kicking the Coal Habit

Coal-burning power plants are the main source of the air pollution that causes acid rain. Every year, the power plants of the world puff out more than 66 million tons of sulfur dioxides into the air through their smokestacks.

Many years ago, the air around the power plants was extremely polluted. Then, the power companies had an idea. They made their smokestacks much taller — as tall as skyscrapers — and the smoke just blew away with the wind. But this didn't really solve the problem. The wind just blew the pollution into somebody else's air.

To stop acid rain, power plants need to cut back on pollution, not just send it farther away. One way to do this is to clean the smoke before it comes out of the smokestacks. This is done with machines called scrubbers. In many countries, such as Japan, all new power plants and factories must be built with scrubbers. Many old plants, however, do not have scrubbers yet because they are costly to install.

London's Killer Smog

When too much pollution collects in the air, it can be dangerous. In 1952, weather patterns over the city of London prevented smoke from coal fires from blowing away. The smoke mixed with fog. Londoners invented a new word for it: smog. The thick smog made breathing almost impossible. More than 4,000 people suffocated from breathing in this polluted air.

from *The Acid Rain Hazard* by Judith Woodburn. Milwaukee: Gareth Stevens Publishing, 1992. P. 19.

On the Surface

1 What is the main source of air pollution causing acid rain? _____

_____

2 How many tons of sulphur dioxide are puffed into the air each year? _____

_____

3 In order to stop acid rain, what do power plants need to do? _____

_____

_____

4 Why don't old power plants have scrubbers? _____

_____

Discoveries

1 Find out about acid rain. Write a brief summary of your findings. _____

_____

_____

2 What is sulfur dioxide? Write a brief explanation. _____

_____

_____

Delving More Deeply

1 Why don't many power companies want to make the change from coal to other sources of energy?

_____

2 What will be the effect of their refusal to change? _____

_____

3 How is smog formed? _____

_____

4 How is smog dangerous to people? Give an example of when this has happened.

_____

_____

5 How did power companies clear up the pollution around the power plants?

_____

Hidden Depths

1 Have you ever been in a city with bad smog? Write an account of how it felt. If not, which cities in the world would you expect to have very bad smog? Why?

_____

_____

_____

2 Write a letter to the president, giving your thoughts on coal-burning power plants.

_____

_____

_____

_____

Extend Yourself

- Find out about the Kyoto Protocol. (You can search on the Internet or do a newspaper article search.) Is our nation involved in the Protocol?

- Research and present a report on alternative energy sources such as hydroelectric, solar, wind, or wave energy. What are the advantages/disadvantages?

- Research acid rain in the U.S.A. How is the government trying to protect the forests?

LESSON 18 New Job

Cross curriculum Literacy Links: History; Work, Employment and Enterprise, Arts

Text Type	Narrative
Purpose	To tell a story
Structure:	**1** Introduction — who or what, where and when
	2 Complication
	3 Series of events
	4 Resolution
Features	Use of past tense, pronouns

from Work: A Story of Experience

A frail, tea-colored lady appeared, displaying such a small proportion of woman to such a large proportion of purple and fine linen, that she looked as if she was literally as well as figuratively "dressed to death."

Christie went to the point in a business-like manner that seemed to suit Mrs. Saltonstall, because it saved so much trouble, and she replied, with a languid affability:

"I wish some one to teach the children a little, for they are getting too old to be left entirely to nurse. I am anxious to get to the sea-shore as soon as possible, for they have been poorly all winter, and my own health has suffered. Do you feel inclined to try the place? And what compensation do you require?"

Christie had but a vague idea of what wages were usually paid to nursery governesses, and hesitatingly named a sum which seemed reasonable to her, but was so much less that any other applicant had asked, that Mrs. Saltonstall began to think she could not do better than secure this cheap young person, who looked firm enough to manage her rebellious son and heir, and well-bred enough to begin the education of a fine little lady. Her winter had been an extravagant one, and she could economize in the governess better than elsewhere; so she decided to try Christie, and get out of town at once.

"Your terms are quite satisfactory, Miss Devon, and if my brother approves, I think we will consider the matter settled. Perhaps you would like to see the children? They are little darlings, and you will soon be fond of them, I'm sure."

A bell was rung, an order given, and presently appeared an eight-year-old boy, so excessively Scotch in his costume that he looked like an animated checker-board; and a little girl, who presented the appearance of a miniature opera-dancer staggering under the weight of an immense sash.

"Go and speak prettily to Miss Devon, my pets, for she is coming to play with you, and you must mind what she says," commanded mamma.

The pale, fretful-looking little pair went solemnly to Christie's knee, and stood there staring at her with a dull composure that quite daunted her, it was so sadly unchildlike.

"What is your name, dear?" she asked, laying her hand on the young lady's head.

"Villamena Temmatine Taltentall. You mustn't touch my hair; it's just been turled," was the somewhat embarrassing reply.

from *Work: A Story of Experience* by Louisa May Alcott. New York: Schocken, 1977.
Originally published 1873. Pp. 59–61.

On the Surface

1 What are the names of the woman applying for the job and the woman interviewing her?

_____

2 What kind of job are they discussing? _____

_____

3 How are the children dressed? _____

_____

4 Why does the little girl complain when her hair is touched? _____

_____

Discoveries

1 Define these words from the passage.

   a poorly _____

   b economize _____

   c fretful _____

   d composure _____

   e daunted _____

2 Why does the little girl give her last name as "Taltentall"? _____

_____

Delving More Deeply

1 Why did Mrs. Saltonstall hire Christie Devon rather than someone else?

_____

_____

2 What does it mean that Mrs. Saltonstall decides to "economize in the governess better perhaps than elsewhere"?

_____

_____

3 What does the little girl's name tell you about this family? _____

_____

_____

4 Why does "mamma" dress her children so ridiculously? _____

_____

_____

Hidden Depths

1 Why do you think Christie is willing to take this job minding two odd, spoiled children?

_____

_____

2 Have you ever taken care of younger children? What challenges are involved?

_____

_____

_____

Extend Yourself

- Research the job of governess, a job that is rarely seen today. What kinds of women took these jobs? What was their experience like? Report your findings to your classmates.

- Write the next scene in the story, in which Christie teaches her first lesson to Wilhelmina and her big brother Louie Napoleon Saltonstall.

- Create drawings or watercolors of Mrs. Saltonstall and her children, drawing on the descriptions in the text and on books that show fashion from the 1870s.

NAME _____   DATE _____

Summer Fun

Cross-Curriculum Literacy Link: Health

Text Type	Advertisement
Purpose	To persuade by putting forward an argument or particular point of view
Structure	1 Images
	2 Written or spoken language
	3 Sensory appeal, e.g., layout, graphics
Features	May include images, facts and figures, logical reasoning, examples, persuasive or emotive language

CAMP SUNRAY — THE PLACE FOR YOUNG ATHLETES!

"CAMP SUNRAY is where I discovered my athletic potential and learned how to reach it!" — Sally Summers, World-Class Swimmer

CAMP SUNRAY is THE place for your young athlete this summer! We offer camps in tennis, swimming, and soccer. Two weeks of outdoor fun and expert guidance by our professional coaches will help your child

✓ master techniques!   ✓ meet new friends!

✓ reach fitness goals!   ✓ make life-long memories!

CAMP SUNRAY offers six summer camp sessions:

June 6–June 18	Intermediate Soccer Skills
June 20–July 1	Tennis Singles
July 5–July 16	Intermediate Swimming and Diving
July 18–July 29	Advanced Soccer Skills
August 1–August 12	Tennis Doubles
August 15–August 26	Advanced Swimming and Life-Saving Skills

Visit our web site for costs and registration forms.

CAMP SUNRAY invites coaches who inspire, encourage, and motivate your young athlete to be the best he or she can be! Coaches' profiles are available at our web site.

CAMP SUNRAY is located within easy driving distance east of Dallas/Ft. Worth, in beautiful Piney Woods, Texas. Shuttles from DFW International Airport are available. Maps available at our web site.

Parents are welcome to visit their children at Camp SunRay. Come eat in our newly remodeled cafeteria, where our chefs prepare nutritious food that keeps young athletes' bodies healthy and full of energy!

CAMP SUNRAY — where your young athlete will shine!

On the Surface

1 With what slogan does the brochure close? _____

_____

2 What information is available at the camp's web site?

_____

3 How many sessions does the camp offer? _____

4 What sports and skills do the camp's coaches teach? _____

_____

Discoveries

1 To what emotions does the writer of the flyer appeal? _____

_____

_____

2 How often does the flyer use exclamation points? Why does it make such frequent use of that mark?

_____

Delving More Deeply

1 Why does the flyer open with a quote from a world-class swimmer? _____

_____

_____

2 How often do the words *Camp SunRay* appear on the flyer? What is the purpose of this repetition?

_____

_____

3 Which of the experiences that children will have at camp are not fitness-related?

_____

4 Why might parents visit their children while they are at camp? _____

_____

_____

Hidden Depths

1   Does this flyer make you want to attend this camp or a similar camp? Explain.

_____

_____

_____

2   Who is the audience for this advertisement? What groups in society might this advertisement not appeal to?

_____

_____

_____

Extend Yourself

• Write your own advertisement for a summer camp, either real or invented. Identify your target audience and consider what language and graphics will appeal to them.

• Visit web sites for summer camps, and analyze what they have in common. What makes a web site easy to use and inviting?

• Discuss with your classmates whether our culture places too much, enough, or too little emphasis on athletics for young people.

LESSON 20 Energy and the World

Cross-Curriculum Literacy Links: Science; Civics and Citizenship

Text Type   Argument

Purpose   To persuade by putting forward an argument or particular point of view

Structure   1 Statement of point of view
2 Justifications of argument in a logical order
3 Summing up of argument

Features   Includes facts and figures, logical reasoning, examples, persuasive or emotive language

The Quest for Clean Energy

Research into how we are to meet the world's growing energy needs without increasing global warming must begin now. Fifty years from now the planet will need three times the amount of energy now generated by using coal, oil and other fossil fuels.

The use of fossil fuels will need to be reduced dramatically, as they generate heat-trapping greenhouse gases which increase global warming.

Scientists have warned us the research effort needs to be equivalent to the Apollo project to put man on the moon. The Apollo project fulfilled President Kennedy's promise to put a man on the moon within 10 years. Millions of dollars were poured into this project during the 1960s, which accelerated the development of technology by decades. Just think of how different the world would be today if this mammoth effort hadn't been made.

According to a current research team of 18 scientists from academic, federal and private research centers, many options need to be explored. Improving existing technologies and developing others such as fusion reactors or space-based solar power plants are suggestions they have made. Scientists say most energy technologies currently in existence either require research and development or are simply inadequate.

This assessment contrasts with the analysis made last year by the Intergovernmental Project on Climate Change, an international panel working under the Industrialized Nations. That analysis concluded that existing technologies such as solar panels, new nuclear power options, windmills, and filters for fossil fuel emissions would be climate-friendly and solve most of the problem.

Dr. Haroon S. Kheshgi, a chemical engineer for Exxon Mobil, is one author of the new analysis. He said that "climate change is a serious risk" and requires a shift away from fossil fuels. "You need a quantum jump in technology," he said. "What we're talking about here is a 50 to 100 year time scale."

Europe and Japan have signed a climate treaty, the Kyoto Protocol, which involves meeting deadlines for cuts in gas emissions. However, not all industrialized nations support it. In addition, leaders of some developing countries have rejected proposed cuts on their fast-growing use of fossil fuels. These leaders believe that industrialized countries — which consume about 80 percent of the world's energy — should act first.

Western, industrialized countries need to make research into climate-friendly energy a priority. Money needs to be poured into projects to find climate-friendly, sustainable energy sources. The future of the world's environment is at stake!

On the Surface

1 In fifty years' time how much energy will the world need? _____

_____

2 How is energy generated now? _____

_____

3 What do these fossil fuels generate? _____

_____

4 If we continue to use fossil fuels, scientists are concerned about the increase in what?

_____

5 What options do the scientific researchers believe need to be explored?

_____

_____

Discoveries

1 Write the meanings of the following words.

   a quest _____

   b consume _____

   c developing _____

   d industrialized _____

2 Connotations are the extra meanings we suggest when we use certain words. What are the connotations of the word *clean* in this text?

_____

Delving More Deeply

1   Which project in the 1960s was so well funded it advanced technological research by decades?

_____

2   According to the article, are most existing technologies going to be adequate for future generations? Explain.

_____

_____

3   Study paragraph 6. Does Dr. Kheshgi support the "50 to 100 year time scale"? Explain.

_____

_____

4   Why do you think the developing countries believe that the industrialized countries should act first?

_____

_____

Hidden Depths

1   Is this article an example of informative writing, persuasive writing, or both? Explain.

_____

_____

_____

2   Why do you think that people who were willing to invest in the Apollo program might not be as willing to invest in exploring new energy sources?

_____

_____

_____

Extend Yourself

•   Find out what the current situation is with the Kyoto Protocol.

•   Find out about the space-based solar panels that might beam energy to Earth using microwaves. Show in a diagram how this could be done.

•   Find out about new fusion-based power plants.

LESSON 21 Heads, You Win

Cross-Curriculum Literacy Links: History; Civics and Citizenship

Text Type	Procedure/Instructions
Purpose	To give instructions or show how something is accomplished through a series of steps
Structure	1 Opening statement of goal or aim
	2 Materials required listed in order of use
	3 Series of steps listed in order
Features	Logical sequence of steps; may use technical language and diagrams

How to Play Two-Up

Players: any number can play
Age: mainly adults
Equipment: two coins and a flat piece of wood for throwing. Historically played with two pennies. The piece of wood was called a kip.

Two-up was a popular game for many years in Australia. The game could be played almost anywhere because it required very little equipment.

Today you will find two-up in games and souvenir shops. Two-up is sold in souvenir sets of old pennies and a wooden kip.

The game of two-up is run by the "boxer," who is in charge of the spinning of the pennies.

The person who spins the coins is known as the "spinner." The spinner tries to throw heads, and the other players in the game guess whether the spinner will succeed.

How to Play

1   The spinner places two pennies on the flat piece of wood, known as the kip. The boxer notifies the spinner to begin by calling "Come in, spinner." The spinner throws the coins.

2   If the pennies are both heads-up, the spinner has won. He loses if they are both tails. If the pennies show one head, one tails, then the throw is declared a no-throw and the spinner repeats the throw.

3   The spinner keeps throwing if heads come up. Heads must turn up three times before the spinner wins. This player can choose to play again or retire and the next spinner will step in.

4   If playing this at home, you can score how many times each player wins a round. This may be the best out of three or five rounds.

On the Surface

1   How many people can play the game of two-up at the same time? _____

_____

2   List the equipment needed. _____

_____

3   Where can you find two-up sets today? _____

_____

4   What is the "boxer" in charge of? _____

_____

Discoveries

1   Write the meanings of the following words.

   a   spectators _____

   b   retire _____

2   Make a list of the terms used in the game of two-up. Give your own definitions for the meanings of these words (e.g., boxer).

_____

_____

3   Why are instructions often provided in a numbered list? _____

_____

Delving More Deeply

1   Explain the role of the spinner. _____

_____

2   What do the other players do? _____

_____

3   Who gets the point if the spinner throws tails? _____

_____

www.harcourtschoolsupply.com   **70**   **Lesson 21**
Reading Comprehension Across the Genres 7, SV 1419023624

4 What needs to happen for the spinner to win? _____

_____

5 How can the scoring be done at home? _____

_____

_____

Hidden Depths

1 Which role would you most like to play in this game? Explain. _____

_____

_____

_____

2 List as many games as you can think of that are similar to two-up. They need to involve chance or probability.

_____

_____

_____

Extend Yourself

- Play a game of two-up with some friends.
- Present a demonstration to the class on how to play the game. Then play a few rounds.
- Invent a new game of chance that is similar to two-up. Write the rules, and demonstrate the game for the class.

Four-Legged Friends

Cross-Curriculum Literacy Links: Science; Civics and Citizenship

Text Type   Discussion

Purpose   To inform and persuade by presenting evidence and opinions about more than one side of an issue

Structure   1 Opening statement presenting the issue
  2 Arguments or evidence for different points of view
  3 Concluding recommendation

Features   Facts and figures, logical reasoning, examples, persuasive or emotive language

Spay or Neuter Your Pet!

You know that, as a pet owner, you are responsible for your pet's well-being. You make sure your cat gets her shots. You feed your pet the right food, and not too much of it. You take your perky little dog for walks twice a day. But you may be overlooking one important health consideration: spaying or neutering your pet. Getting your pet "fixed" is important for your pet's health and for the health of other animals as well.

Spaying female pets or neutering male pets removes their reproductive organs so that the pets cannot have offspring. You may think at first that these procedures sound cruel, but they are not. In fact, the procedures are simple and done under anesthesia, and the animal recovers quickly. Better still, spaying and neutering increase the chances of your beloved pet living a long and healthy life.

A spayed or neutered animal has less chance of developing certain cancers and infections. These animals also behave more safely. Neutered male cats and dogs are less likely to roam, get lost, or engage in fights over other females. All animals are safer the closer they stay to home, because they avoid contact with animals that have infectious diseases such as feline leukemia, which is often fatal.

A spayed or neutered animal is also a better behaved animal at home. Neutered males will not spray your furniture to mark their territory, and they will be less aggressive toward other male animals. Spayed females do not experience heats, inconvenient spells of annoying mating behaviors.

Some pet owners worry that their pets will become fat and lazy if they are neutered or spayed. This is a myth. Good pet owners make sure that their animals get enough exercise and eat a healthy diet. Overfeeding and lack of exercise lead to overweight animals, not neutering and spaying. Overweight animals live shorter lives, while fixed animals live on average two or three years longer than pets that have not been spayed or neutered.

There is a greater reason to have your pet neutered or spayed. Every year, millions of kittens and puppies are born but find no loving homes to take them in. Animal shelters are full of homeless animals, most of which must eventually be euthanized. Other litters are born stray and die of starvation or die by accident. When you are responsible for your pet by having her spayed, you are preventing the suffering of other animals.

Spaying and neutering are simple, inexpensive procedures. If your pet hasn't had them yet, call your vet today.

On the Surface

1 According to the article, what responsibilities do pet owners have?

_____

_____

2 How do the spaying and neutering procedures affect animals' ability to reproduce?

_____

3 What endangers unneutered male dogs and cats? _____

_____

4 What myth about spaying and neutering does the article address? _____

_____

Discoveries

1 Write the meanings of the following words.

a consideration _____

b litter _____

c mark _____

d myth _____

e euthanized _____

2 List the evidence used in this piece. _____

_____

_____

_____

Delving More Deeply

1 Why might pet owners want their cat or dog to produce a litter? _____

_____

_____

2 To what emotions does the writer of the article appeal? _____

_____

_____

_____

3 How will spaying or neutering change pets' behavior?

  a Pets will become less aggressive towards other animals.

  b Pets will not be as loving as they were before the procedure.

4 Where do you think the writer would suggest a person go to get a new pet?

  a To an animal shelter to choose a homeless animal

  b To a breeder to buy an expensive animal

Hidden Depths

1 Do you know anyone who has refused to have his or her pet spayed or neutered? What are his or her reasons for forgoing the procedure? Explain.

_____

_____

2 List several legitimate reasons for allowing dogs and cats to have litters.

_____

_____

_____

Extend Yourself

• A new non-surgical procedure has been developed for neutering male dogs. Research this procedure on the Internet or by interviewing a vet. Then report on the procedure to your classmates.

• Visit your community's animal shelter, and talk to the shelter's managers and volunteers about the importance of spaying and neutering. Make a photo journal or mini-documentary of your experience to share with your classmates.

LESSON ⟨23⟩ Hard Times

Cross-Curriculum Literacy Links: Difference and Diversity; Civics and Citizenship; History

Text Type	Cartoon
Purpose	To entertain and/or make a social comment
Structure	1 Image or series of images usually in the form of line drawings
	2 Written or spoken language accompanying images
Features	Visual and language cues to convey meanings at multiple levels; may be related to current affairs or issues

Old-Timer Tells Tall Tale

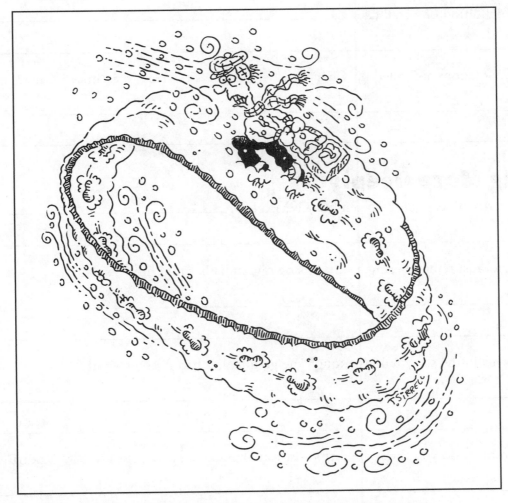

Yes, your grandfather could have walked three miles to school
through the snow uphill both ways.

Reading Comprehension Across the Genres 7, SV 1419023624

On the Surface

1   Whose grandfather is referred to in the cartoon? _____

_____

2   What does the cartoon's title call the grandfather? _____

_____

3   Who is the person shown in the cartoon? _____

_____

4   Who is the speaker of the cartoon's caption? _____

_____

Discoveries

1   Write a definition of a "tall tale." _____

_____

2   What connotations are called up when an older person is referred to as an old-timer?

_____

_____

Delving More Deeply

1   Can the cartoon's caption be taken literally? Explain. _____

_____

2   Is the cartoonist remembering a story his own grandfather told him? Explain.

_____

_____

3   What details in the story tell how tough the grandfather had it in his youth?

_____

_____

4   What comment do you think the cartoonist is making about some stories that grandparents tell?

_____

_____

Reading Comprehension Across the Genres 7, SV 1419023624

Hidden Depths

1   What exaggerated story has an older person told you about the tough times of his or her youth? Why do you think he or she told you that story?

_____

_____

_____

2   What is a Möbius strip, and why has the cartoonist used one to express the idea of the cartoon?

_____

_____

_____

_____

Extend Yourself

•   What amazing or inspiring stories do we keep telling about important historical figures, such as the story of George Washington throwing a silver dollar across the Delaware River? Why are these stories important to our culture, even if they're not entirely true? Collect such stories and discuss their functions with your classmates.

•   Imagine that you are describing your own teen years to your future grandchildren. Write an exaggerated account of how hard you had it.

•   Illustrate your story, and add it to other classmates' stories and illustrations to create a humorous booklet about teens' lives in the early 21st century.

LESSON 24 A New Take on Nutrition

Cross-Curriculum Literacy Links: History; Civics and Citizenship

Text Type	Newspaper article
Purpose	To persuade by putting forward an argument or particular point of view
Structure	**1** Statement of point of view
	2 Justifications of argument in a logical order
	3 Summing up of argument
Features	Facts and figures, logical reasoning, examples, persuasive or emotional language

Government Introduces New Food Pyramid

You may have learned, back in elementary school, about the food pyramid. It had layers, with grains on the bottom and sugars and fats at the very tip. This pyramid reminded you to eat breads and cereals for fiber and to limit your sugar intake. But now that pyramid is, like those crumbling Egyptian monuments, history. Four years and over 2 million dollars have gone into making a new food pyramid, which the United States Department of Agriculture has just released.

The new pyramid is better in many ways. First, it is based on more up-to-date science. Nutritionists understand more about the body and the way it uses food than they used to. Also, the pyramid now does more than remind people of what they should eat and how much they should eat of it. It also features a person climbing stairs, to remind people that

they need to exercise daily. Best of all, the pyramid no longer stands alone. It's supported by a Web site, mypyramid.gov, free to anyone who wants to use it, that explains how to eat a healthy diet. You can enter your age, weight, height, and activity level to get a personalized food and exercise plan.

Not everyone is entirely happy with the USDA's new pyramid, however. Some critics say that, while the pyramid is more colorful to look at, it's harder to interpret. The old pyramid had horizontal bars, with the foods you should eat more of at the bottom and the foods you should limit in a small triangle at the top. Today's pyramid is split into vertical wedges that are supposed to suggest good portion sizes of food. But it's not easy to tell, for instance, whether vegetables or dairy is more important. (Bad news for chocolate fans

— sweets are nowhere on the new pyramid!)

Other critics say that the pyramid doesn't guide people to eat whole grains — such as oats — rather than refined grains. The body digests whole grains slowly, but it treats refined grains — such as white bread — almost the same as sugar.

Most important to some critics is the lack of words on the new pyramid. People have to remember what each color band stands for — but why is dairy blue? People can visit the Web site to get the text that explains the pyramid, but not everyone has access to the Internet.

Despite its shortcomings, the new pyramid is a better way to help people choose good foods. And that little stick guy hiking up the stairs may just get people up and moving!

On the Surface

1 What has just been introduced? _____

_____

2 Why are the new guidelines needed? _____

_____

_____

3 Where can people learn about the new guidelines? _____

_____

4 Other than recommending types and portions of food, what do the new guidelines advise?

_____

Discoveries

1 Write the meanings of the following words.

    a intake _____

    b nutritionists _____

    c interpret _____

    d refined _____

    e shortcomings _____

2 Why do news articles often feature short paragraphs? _____

_____

_____

Delving More Deeply

1 What do critics find wrong with the new pyramid? _____

_____

_____

2 Why did it take four years and over 2 million dollars to develop the new pyramid?

_____

_____

3 Why do people need graphics such as the food pyramid? _____

_____

_____

4 What help does the Web site, mypyramid.gov, offer to anyone who needs it?

_____

_____

Hidden Depths

1 What diet fads have you heard or read about? Do these diet fads follow the guidelines of the new pyramid? Explain.

_____

_____

_____

2 Would you use the information available at mypyramid.gov? Explain. _____

_____

_____

_____

Extend Yourself

- Visit mypyramid.gov. Report to your classmates about the guidance the site offers.
- Download a poster of the new pyramid at the Web site, and interpret it for your classmates.
- Design your own graphic to promote a healthy diet, based on the guidelines at mypyramid.gov.

LESSON 25 Pop Psychology

Cross-Curriculum Literacy Links: Gender; Difference and Diversity; Health

Text Type Magazine article (Quiz)
Purpose To entertain and inform
Structure 1 Introduction — background information about who, where, and when
          2 Series of events in chronological order
          3 A personal comment
Features Past tense, action verbs, descriptive language; may include quotes

The True You

Think you know yourself pretty well? Follow the trail of questions to discover more about who you really are . . .

1 You wake up in the morning and throw on your favorite top. The color of the top is:
   a red   e green
   b baby pink f blue
   c orange   g purple
   d yellow   h white

2 You close the door behind you and head off. You'll be:
   a jogging most of the way
   b walking briskly
   c strolling

3 You've got a small backpack with you. You carry the backpack:
   a on both shoulders
   b slung over one shoulder

4 You walk towards your fave spot near the water. The water is:
   a the crashing surf of an ocean beach
   b a flowing river, bubbling over rocks and pebbles
   c a still lake, surrounded by sloping banks of reeds

5 You notice a bridge you've never seen before. You:
   a wonder where it leads, but keep going on your way
   b divert from your route, and follow the bridge to wherever it goes
   c walk over for a look, but stay on your set path

6 You make yourself comfortable next to a particular tree. The tree is:
   a a tall, leafy tree with branches that spread high into the sky
   b a weeping willow with long limbs trailing on the grass
   c a low shrub with large leaves and pretty white flowers

7 Sitting down to relax with a book, you choose to:
   a lie on your back with your head resting on a grassy tuft
   b sit up, leaning back with your legs in front and bent
   c sit cross-legged and straight-backed

8 While sitting near the water you see your favorite animal. List three things you love about this animal:
   _____

9 Near the water is a beautiful house. It's:
   a on top of a grassy hill with no fence and a view of the water
   b tucked into a sheltered hillside, with a large garden leading to the water
   c nestled in a section of forest surrounded by a fenced garden

10 At the front of the house is a fountain. You see its shape as:
    a circular
    b square or diamond

11 As you approach the house, people appear at the front door. You decide to:
    a quickly turn and walk away, hoping they don't see you
    b signal or wave, and approach them to explain that you're just looking at the fountain

12 You decide to head home. There are two routes—along the road, which is quicker, or along the water, the way you came. Which one do you take?
    a the longer route — you're in no rush
    b the shorter route — there's no point in dawdling when you can go directly home

Dolly Magazine, ACP Syndication, Sydney, December 2002, P. 135

On the Surface

1   The quiz is based on a journey. List the activities you undertake on the journey.

_____

_____

2   Which question gives you the most range of choices? _____

_____

3   Which question involves a decision which may lead you off your path?

_____

4   Where do you make yourself comfortable? _____

_____

Discoveries

1   Write definitions for the following words.

   a extroverted   _____

   b ambitious   _____

   c sympathetic   _____

   d vital   _____

   e aspiring   _____

   f spontaneous   _____

2   What might a person's choice of the route home, in question 12, mean about that person?

_____

_____

_____

Delving More Deeply

1   What do the colors symbolize? _____

_____

2   How do you decide when more than one option is appropriate? _____

_____

3   How you wore the backpack relates to how others see you. List the uses of a bag. What do bags symbolize in this quiz?

_____

_____

_____

4   What do bridges symbolize? _____

_____

Hidden Depths

1   Did you enjoy the activity? Does the text fulfill the purpose of entertainment? Comment on what you learned about yourself.

_____

_____

_____

2   How realistic is this sort of quiz? Should it be taken seriously, or is it just for fun?

_____

_____

_____

Extend Yourself

• Make a poster or booklet called "The True Me." Include a picture of your favorite spot, your favorite animal, and a house you love. Make sure the book is in your favorite color.

• Research quizzes in other magazines for young teens and note what topics they cover.

• Which type of quiz do you like most/least? Why?

• The "answers" to this quiz are not given. Create a score sheet that tells readers what kind of person they are based on their responses to the quiz.

LESSON (26) **Busy Young Scholars**

Cross-Curriculum Literacy Links: Mathematics

Text Type Timetable; Student schedule
Purpose To display information about time, place, and other relevant information efficiently
Structure: Table format using words and numbers
Features Abbreviations

	MON.	TUES.	WED.	THURS.	FRI.
8:40	lang. arts Ms. Kang B Wing 103	lang. arts Ms. Kang B Wing 103	lang. arts Ms. Kang B Wing 103	lang. arts Ms. Kang B Wing 103	lang. arts Ms. Kang B Wing 103
10:15	orchestra Ms. Powers Music Bldg.	orchestra Ms. Powers Music Bldg.	orchestra Ms. Powers Music Bldg.	orchestra Ms. Powers Music Bldg.	cello class Ms. Powers Music Bldg.
11:15	science Ms. Jeffers C Wing lab	social stud. Mr. Medrano B Wing 200	science Ms. Jeffers C Wing lab	social stud. Mr. Medrano B Wing 200	study time Library
12:15	lunch/recess	lunch/recess	lunch/recess	lunch/recess	lunch/recess
12:40	art Mr. Van Dyke A Wing 124	PE Coach Kim Gym	art Mr. Van Dyke A Wing 124	PE Coach Kim Gym	art Mr. Van Dyke A Wing 124
1:35	math Ms. Fife C wing 111	math Ms. Fife C wing 111	math Ms. Fife C wing 111	math Ms. Fife C wing 111	math Ms. Fife C wing 111
2:25	science Ms. Rivas C Wing lab	social stud. Mr. Medrano B Wing 200	science Ms. Rivas C Wing lab	social stud. Mr. Medrano B Wing 200	study time Library
4:00	dismissal	dismissal	dismissal	dismissal	dismissal
4:15	EC: tennis Coach Ely Gym or courts	EC: tennis Coach Ely Gym or courts	EC: tennis Coach Ely Gym or courts	EC: tennis Coach Ely Gym or courts	EC: tennis Coach Ely Gym or courts

On the Surface

1 Which class runs longest at this school? _____
_____

2 How many male teachers does this student have? How many female teachers? Can you be sure?
_____
_____

3 On the schedule, in what order is the information presented?

   a Subject, teacher, room number

   b Teacher, subject, room number

   c Room number, teacher, subject

4 How many wings does the main school building have? _____
_____

Discoveries

1 List some of the topics you would study under the following subject areas.

   a Social Studies _____

   b Language Arts _____

   c PE (Physical Education) _____

   d Art _____

2 What abbreviations does the schedule use? Why are abbreviations helpful on schedules?
_____
_____

Delving More Deeply

1 On Tuesday, which subject does the student have just before lunchtime? _____
_____

2 Who does the student have for math? _____
_____

3 Why might the tennis team meet in the gym rather than on the courts?

_____

_____

4 Is PE different from tennis? Explain. _____

_____

_____

_____

Hidden Depths

1 What academic subjects does the student have every day? Why are these subjects scheduled daily, instead of several times a week, as other subjects are?

_____

_____

_____

2 In some countries, school begins at 8 A.M. and ends at 1 P.M. Students then go home, eat lunch, and do their homework. What do you think of this approach?

_____

_____

_____

Extend Yourself

• Compare your school's schedules to the one above. How are the schedules similar? How are they different?

• Make up your own ideal schedule for one day.

NAME _____   DATE _____

Cross-Curriculum Literacy Links: Geography; Civics and Citizenship

Text Type	Narrative (Autobiography)
Purpose	To tell a story
Structure	1 Introduction — who or what, where and when
	2 Complication
	3 Series of events
	4 Resolution
Features	Use of past tense, pronouns

From Lionheart

Sunday, December 7, 1998

With the genoa unfurled for the first time, I passed Sorrento, then Portsea, making my way through the South Channel to the starting line — the Heads of Port Phillip Bay, the most treacherous port entry and exit in the world.

I cut a thick slice of salami, then rushed up on deck to correct the wandering steering that had once again deviated slightly towards land. Maybe Lionheart was trying to tell me something. Maybe she'd prefer to stay at home in the shelter and safety of the bay rather than enter the unknown of Bass Strait. Did she know we were about to take on the world? Moments later I crossed the line, and my new life began.

What makes a seventeen-year-old decide to sail around the world? I'm not exactly sure; I was actually fourteen when I first started to think about doing so. When I sailed from Port Phillip Bay on 7 December, 1998, the trip was the culmination of years of dreaming.

Others may have thought I was a foolish young man, but I'd been working towards that dream for a long time.

Why? That's the question I get asked most. And one of the reasons behind this book. I don't just want to tell the story of how I sailed around the world on my own, but to reveal why a teenager would want to leave the comfort of home for eleven months at sea, and what I learnt from the experience.

It has been said that every great adventure begins with one small step. It's clichéd, but it's true. I've taken thousands of steps to become the youngest person to sail solo, non-stop and unassisted around the world.

But what was that first step? Was it sailing through the Port Phillip Heads, my official starting point of the trip? Was it waving goodbye to family and friends at the Sandringham Yacht Club? Was it when my major sponsor agreed to commit $160,000 to my trip? Was it that moment, at fourteen years of age, when I first dreamt of sailing around the world? Was it my previous adventures? Was it the first time I stepped aboard a boat? Was it when I was born?

Who knows, but I suspect Mum and Dad had a fair bit to do with it.

from *Lionheart: A Journey of the Human Spirit* by Jesse Martin (with Ed Gannon).
Sydney: Allen & Unwin, 2000. Pp. 3–4.

On the Surface

1 Which is the most treacherous port entry/exit in the world? _____

_____

2 Who or what is *Lionheart?* _____

_____

3 How old was Jesse when he started to think about sailing around the world?

_____

4 What date did Jesse set sail from Port Phillip Bay? _____

_____

5 What else does Jesse want to reveal in the book? _____

_____

Discoveries

1 Write the meanings of the following words.

   a unfurled _____

   b deviated _____

   c culmination _____

   d clichéd _____

2 What is the significance of the name of Jesse's boat, *Lionheart?*

_____

Delving More Deeply

1 Jesse says he's taken thousands of steps to become the youngest person to sail solo around the world. What do you think he means by "thousands"?

_____

2 Who do you think has been the biggest influence on Jesse in this adventure?

_____

3 What will be covered in the book? _____

_____

_____

4 What indicates that Jesse was a bit nervous on his first part of the journey?

_____

5 How did some other people react to his plan to sail solo around the world?

_____

Hidden Depths

1 How would you have felt sailing out through Port Phillip Heads that day?

_____

_____

2 Outline some of the dreams you have had (big or small). How many steps will you need to take to achieve them?

_____

_____

_____

Extend Yourself

- Read the rest of the book.

- Make a web of Jesse Martin's personal qualities.

- Most parents of a teenager wouldn't allow him or her to sail around the world. Write a 500-word personal piece on how people's faith in you builds your confidence. Comment on your faith in your abilities, or comment on what you would like people to have faith in you about.

- It took great courage for Jesse's parents to allow him to go on this journey. Interview your own parents on the bravery it takes sometimes to be a parent, in allowing children to explore the world around them. Write a report on your findings, including a comment on what you have learned from the interview.

LESSON 28 New in Print

Cross-Curriculum Literacy Links: Multicultural Content; Civics and Citizenship

Text Type Web site
Structure Review
  1 Context — background information on the text
  2 Description of the text (including characters and plot).
  3 Concluding statement (judgment, opinion, or recommendation).
Features Language may be formal or informal depending on purpose and audience; may include examples and quotes

Read Any Good Books Lately?

Comments/Review on A Single Shard *by Linda Sue Park*
Written by: Anna
School: Mulberry Middle School
State: Texas

A Single Shard is a beautiful story that made me laugh and then cry. It's so full of hardship overcome and hope kept alive that I felt happier after reading it. I'd really like to see the story of Tree-ear, his guardian Crane-man, and the potter Min brought to life in a movie!! I've never been to Korea, where the story is set, and a movie would make the setting more real to me. I think what I loved best about the story is how loyal Tree-ear is to those who care for him in any way — how he helps Crane-man, does little favors for Min's wife, and carries the single shard over mountains to prove that his master, Min, is a great potter.

Comments from: Sofie, Pickett Junior High, Idaho

Anna's right — this book would make a great movie. But would it ever be a tear-jerker! I cried when I read the book — can't tell you why, or I'd give away the ending. If I saw the story instead of reading it — well, let's just say, "Pass the tissues," and get it over with. I'll remember Tree-ear's dedication and courage 4ever! Plus, I learned a lot about how hard it is 2 make a good pot!!!

Comments from: Brian, Grayson Middle School, Indiana

So far only girls have commented on this book. Don't be misled, guys — there are hardly any girls in the book, only Min's wife, and all she does is cook and clean! This is a book about a boy who figures out what he wants out of life and goes for it, braving disapproval, rejection, and punishment. He doesn't wuss out when things get hard; he just tries harder. It's also a book about dads and sons. Even though Tree-ear never knew his real father, he finds strong, wise men around him to guide him on his journey. This book helped me realize that no challenge is too great if you really want to achieve your dream. And I didn't shed one tear, Anna and Sofie!

> **View 57 other reviews of this book**
> **Add your own comments/review about this book**
> **Recommend a book similar to this one**
> **Back to Read Any Good Books Lately? Index**
> "Read Any Good Books Lately?" at http://ggc.ragbl/
> (not a live site)

On the Surface

1 Which country do these reviews come from? _____

_____

2 What are the comments/review about? _____

_____

3 What is the name of the Web site? _____

_____

4 How many other reviews can you view on this Web site? _____

_____

5 What else can you do on this Web site? _____

_____

Discoveries

1 Write definitions for the following words.

   a guardian _____

   b shard _____

   c braving _____

2 Look at the language Sophie uses in her review. What do 4 and 2 replace?

_____

3 The language of these reviews is informal. List some examples. Add some other examples you may know of this type of language or abbreviation.

_____

_____

Delving More Deeply

1 What type of book is *A Single Shard?* _____

_____

2 Outline the basic story line of the book. _____

_____

_____

3 Why is a Web site a convenient place to read and write reviews of a book?

_____

_____

4 What age group do you think the reviewers are? _____

_____

5 What do the reviewers love about this book? _____

_____

Hidden Depths

1 Do the reviews inspire you to read the book? If so, what in particular attracts you? If not, explain what you don't like about the book.

_____

_____

_____

2 Would you look at a Web site such as this if you were looking for a good book to read? Explain why. If not, where else would you look for reviews?

_____

_____

_____

Extend Yourself

• Read *A Single Shard.* Then write the comments that you would like to add to the Web site.

• Locate similar Web sites, review each one, and post your recommendations for your classmates to use.

• Write your own back cover "blurb" for a novel that you enjoyed reading.

LESSON 29 Entertainment 24/7

Cross-Curriculum Literacy Links: Arts

Text Type Television program guide
Purpose To display information about time, place, and other relevant details efficiently
Structure Table format using words and numbers
Features Abbreviations, technical language

Cable TV

Ovation Channel 43	Hallmark Channel 24	Nickelodeon Channel 5	Cartoon Network Channel 28	Disney Channel 27	BBC World Channel 37
ENTERTAINMENT	**ENTERTAINMENT**	**KIDS**	**KIDS**	**FAMILY**	**NEWS**
7:00 Tom Jones	6:30 Degree of Guilt (Pt 1) (1995)	6:00 The Fox Busters	6:00 The Popeye Show	6:00 Sabrina	News Every Hour
8.00 Art and Inspiration	8:30 Hollywood Squares	6:30 Moose the Vampire	6:30 The Mask	7:00 The Lion King	7:45 Holiday
8:30 Adventures from The Wild West. Travel series.	9:00 A Country Practice (PG)	9:00 Doug Replay from noon.	8:00 A Pup Named Scooby-Doo	7:30 Buzz Lightyear of Star Command	9:30 Asia Business Report
9:00 Living with the Future	10:00 Police Rescue	2:00 Open Sesame	9:00 The Snorks Summer Splash!	8:30 Disney's The Little Mermaid	9:45 World Business Report
10:00 Talking Books. Classics.	11:00 Big Sky (PG)	2:30 Clarissa Explains	10:00 Tom and Jerry Kids	9:00 Rolie Polie Olie	News Every Hour
10:30 The Forsyte Saga. Classic drama series. (PG)	12:00 Degree of Guilt (Pt 1) (1995)	3:00 Saved by the Bell	11:00 The Zoo	9:30 The Book of Pooh	12:30 Asia Today
12:00 Melba (PG)	2:00 The Incident (1990)	3:30 Worst Witch: Weirdsister College	12:00 Scooby & Scrappy-Doo	10:00 Out of the Box	4:30 World Business Report
3:00 Tom Jones	4:00 Hollywood Squares	4:30 Rocket Power	1:00 The Flintstones and Jetsons Hour	10:30 Bear in the Big Blue House	6:45 Sport Today
4:00 Great Lodges of the National Parks	4:30 A Country Practice (PG)	5:00 Rugrats	2:00 The Popeye Show	11:00 Madeline	7:30 Click Online
5:00 An Umbrian Kitchen	5:30 Hollywood Squares	6:00 Mary-Kate and Ashley in Action	3:00 The Tom and Jerry Show	12:00 Rolie Polie Olie	8:30 Earth Report
6:30 The Forsyte Saga. Drama series (PG)	6:30 Police Rescue	7:00 The Incredible Story Studio	4:00 The Looney Tunes Show	1:00 Bear in the Big Blue House	10:30 Hardtalk
8:30 Ruth Rendell Mysteries	7:30 Water Rats	8:00 Taina	5:00 Cardcaptors	2:00 Madeline	News Every Hour
1:30 Trailside Travel Series	8:30 Degree of Guilt (Pt 2) (1995)	9:00 Kennan and Kel	6:00 X-Men Evolution	3:00 Wishbone	
2:30 The Forsyte Saga (PG)	10:30 Journey (1995) Drama	9:30 Are you Afraid of the Dark?	6:30 Justice League	4:00 Sabrina	
	12:30 A Country Practice (PG)	12:30 Aaahh!! Real Monsters	7:00 Johnny Bravo	5:30 The Jersey	
	1:30 Hollywood Squares		7:30 Dexter's Laboratory	7:30 Pete's Dragon (1977)	
			9:00 Dragon Ball	9:30 Parker-Lewis Can't Lose	
			9:30 Dragon Ball	10:00 Muppets Tonight	
			11:30 Mr. T	1:00 The Zack Files	
				2:00 The Gift	

abbreviated from *Foxtel Magazine*, December 2002, P. 107.

Reading Comprehension Across the Genres 7, SV 1419023624

On the Surface

1 List the channels covered on this page of the guide. _____

_____

_____

2 List how the entertainment, family, and news channels are divided up. _____

_____

3 How many channels cater for children? List them. _____

_____

4 How often does BBC World broadcast news? _____

_____

5 Which channels repeat programs on the same day? _____

_____

Discoveries

1 What does the abbreviation PG stand for in film classifications? _____

_____

2 Find other classifications and write what they stand for. _____

_____

_____

Delving More Deeply

1 List the areas of interest covered by BBC World. _____

_____

2 Find out what BBC stands for. _____

_____

3 Why do you think the Disney Channel is classified as a family channel, not a children's channel? Give some examples of family programs.

_____

_____

94

4   Which entertainment channel has more programming that is informative or artistic?

_____

Hidden Depths

1   Is there a program you are really interested in watching? Explain why. _____

_____

_____

_____

2   Which channel do you think is the best? Explain why. _____

_____

_____

_____

Extend Yourself

•   Develop your own channel guide. Give your channel a name. Schedule your favorite programs, films, etc. (Try to have variety and be aware of scheduling certain programs for certain times of the day for a particular audience.)

•   Discussion: Which films do you tend to watch? In which genre would you classify them? (Action, romance, mystery, etc.)

•   Discussion: Do you think it is worth paying extra money for cable television? Explain why or why not.

LESSON 30 Rating the Movies

Cross-Curriculum Literacy Links: Arts; Civics and Citizenship

Text Type   Response, film review
Purpose   To review a text
Structure   1 Review
                2 Context — background information on the text
                3 Description of the text (including characters and plot)
                4 Concluding statement (judgment, opinion, or recommendation)
Features   Language may be formal or informal depending on purpose and audience; may include examples and quotes

Holes

How many times have you seen a movie made from a favorite book — and then wished you hadn't? Sometimes it almost seems as if the plot and characters of the book were only an afterthought in the movie director's mind. Maybe the movie's great, too, but you're left wondering why the book's story had to be changed. After all, if it's not broken, why fix it?

Some readers — myself included — worried that they might feel just this way when they saw the movie *Holes*, based on Louis Sachar's award-winning novel. But thanks to close cooperation between Sachar and the movie's director and cast, *Holes* doesn't disappoint even the most demanding of viewers.

Filmed in the unforgiving desert of west Texas, *Holes* introduces Shia LeBouef in the starring role of Stanley Yelnats. Sigourney Weaver is the frightening, rattlesnake-venom wielding Warden. Jon Voight and Tim Blake Nelson round out the team of abusive camp counselors, Mr. Sir and Mr. Pendanski, at Camp Greenlake, where digging holes builds character. These and other cast members *become* the characters of the book; their faces and voices will stay in the minds of readers as they enjoy the book again. The score, too, is effective, moving viewers seamlessly from the present scenes to the Greenlake of a hundred years ago — when there actually was a lake — and even further back in Latvia, when Stanley's family fell under a dreadful curse.

Just remember what Mr. Sir says, viewers: "This ain't no Girl Scout camp." Yellow-spotted lizards, shovels, dust storms, and thirst plague the inmates at Camp Greenlake, and the movie makes these trials nearly tangible. After the movie, we headed straight for the nearest water fountain, desperately grateful for plentiful cool water. *Holes* really brings Sachar's beloved book to life — so take a large drink with you when you see it!

Rating:	PG	Time:	117 Minutes
Country:	United States of America	Director:	Andrew Davis
Cast:	Sigourney Weaver, Jon Voight,		
	Tim Blake Nelson, Patricia Arquette,		
	Shia LaBeouf		
Distributor:	Walt Disney		

On the Surface

1 What film is being reviewed here and who directed it? _____

_____

2 Who wrote the book on which the movie is based? _____

_____

3 List three factors that contributed to this film's success. _____

_____

_____

4 Who are the five main actors in this film? _____

_____

_____

Discoveries

1 Who might be the intended audience for this film review? _____

_____

_____

2 Highlight difficult vocabulary and make a class word bank. Investigate and discuss the meaning of different words and ideas. Share and discuss.

3 Underline the adjectives or describing words in the text. Share and discuss.

Delving More Deeply

1 Who are the "bad guys" in the movie's conflict? _____

_____

2 What might have been challenging about the filming location of *Holes?* _____

_____

_____

3 Why was the reviewer worried at first that she wouldn't enjoy the movie?

_____

4 What physical effect did the movie have on the reviewer? _____

_____

Hidden Depths

1 Must films based on books be true to the books' plots? What are some movies based on books that improve on the books' plots?

_____

_____

_____

2 What are some reasons that a director may choose to change a book's plot and characters when making a film?

_____

_____

_____

_____

Extend Yourself

- View the film *Holes*. Discuss whether digging holes builds character.

- Write a review of the film *Holes* with a partner.

- Read the book, and discuss with classmates whether you agree with the reviewer that the movie follows the book closely.

- Design a film poster for *Holes*.

- Collect film reviews and read them aloud as if for television presentation. Do written reviews need to be modified for this different mode of communication? What other cues could assist in a television review?

LESSON 31 Writer and Director

Cross-Curriculum Literacy Links: History; Arts; Work, Employment and Enterprise

Text Type	Account
Purpose	To reconstruct past experiences by telling events
Structure	1 Background information about who, where, and when
	2 Series of events in chronological order
	3 A personal comment (optional)
Features	Use of past tense, action verbs, descriptive language; may include quotes

Digging the Perfect Hole: Louis Sachar and Andrew Davis Collaborate to Make a Great Movie from a Great Book

Film director Andrew Davis comes from a family of actors and a background of theater experience. He's also studied journalism — so he knows a good story when he hears one. Louis Sachar's *Holes* is that kind of story — a "great heartfelt story," Davis says, that is "intelligent and doesn't talk down to kids." Davis's children loved the novel, too, so Davis knew he had a hit on his hands when he approached Sachar about making the movie.

For Sachar, turning his award-winning novel into a screenplay was a new and challenging experience. "The hardest thing for me in writing a screenplay," he says, "was learning to tell a story in pictures and not words." Even though the story didn't change much from book to movie, Sachar worked through four drafts before he was satisfied with the screenplay; and even then, he and Andrews made changes to the script during shooting.

Sachar doesn't worry about writing many drafts of a novel or a screenplay — he's used to working through lots of drafts before the story is as good as it can be. Still, in the hot, dusty desert of west Texas, filming was challenging and time was short. Sachar stayed on the set, available to work out last-minute glitches in the script with the actors.

Sachar and Davis cite their experience in making *Holes* to encourage kids to explore their own creativity. For writer and director, the story is the most important thing, even if it takes hard work to get it down. Kids who'd like to make movies some day should learn all the skills involved — filming, creating sets, casting characters — but "writing is the real important part of it," Davis says. He gets story ideas from events and people in his life who have made an impact on him. When kids ask Sachar where he gets his story ideas, he advises them to start writing anything. "I find the best ideas come while I'm writing. I may start with something and as I'm writing it leads to another idea and then to another idea and that's the idea I get excited about." It worked for *Holes*, and it can work for young writers as well.

On the Surface

1 Who collaborated on the movie *Holes?* _____

_____

2 What is Davis's background? _____

_____

3 Where was *Holes* filmed? _____

_____

4 How can we tell which words Andrew Davis or Louis Sachar actually said in the article?

_____

Discoveries

1 How does using words actually spoken by the director and writer strengthen the article?

_____

_____

2 The article says that Davis "knew he had a hit on his hands" with Sachar's story. What effect does the alliteration (the repetition of the initial *h* sounds) in this sentence have?

_____

_____

Delving More Deeply

1 Why did Andrew Davis think Sachar's novel would make a good movie?

_____

_____

2 What do the many drafts of the screenplay tell readers about how writers work?

_____

_____

3 What major difference did Sachar discover between writing a novel and writing a screenplay?

_____

_____

4 What does Davis mean when he says that the novel *Holes* "doesn't talk down to kids"?

_____

_____

_____

Hidden Depths

1 How can sitting down to write without a good story idea in mind lead to a good story idea, as Sachar says it does for him?

_____

_____

_____

2 What does a screenplay look like, and how is it quite different from the format of a novel? Find a screenplay to examine.

_____

_____

Extend Yourself

• The novel *Holes* won the Newbery Award, along with many other awards. Find out what the Newbery Award is, and read Sachar's acceptance speech. Report your findings to the class.

• Sachar has written many other books, in the *Marvin Post* and *Wayside School* series. Read another of his books and discuss it in comparison with *Holes*.

NAME _____   DATE _____

"He Was About This Tall"

Cross-Curriculum Literacy Links: Civics and Citizenship

Text Type Form
Purpose To record information
Structure Highly structured, logical format with formalized questions and answers
Features Abbreviations, technical or legal language, visual information, a range of fonts

Suspicious Incident Form

Stay Safe

This information could help police to solve a crime.

Location of incident _____

Time _____   Date _____

What did you witness? _____

_____

SUSPICIOUS PERSON

Sex   M   F   Height _____

Build
☐ Thin (Slender)
☐ Medium
☐ Muscular
☐ Solid
☐ Overweight
☐ Obese (very overweight)

Hair color
☐ Fair
☐ Gray
☐ Light Brown
☐ Dark Brown
☐ Red
☐ Black
☐ Dyed   Explain _____

Hair Style
☐ Short
☐ Long
☐ Curly
☐ Straight
☐ Balding
☐ Bald

Eye Color
☐ Gray
☐ Hazel
☐ Green
☐ Blue
☐ Brown
☐ Black

Complexion
☐ Sallow
☐ Pale
☐ Medium
☐ Olive
☐ Dark

Facial Hair
☐ Moustache
☐ Beard
☐ Other   Explain _____

Clothing	Tattoos/Scars
Upper body _____	_____
Lower body _____	_____

Have you seen this person before? Y   N

If so, where/when? _____

Last sighted _____

Direction person headed in _____

On the Surface

1   List the information that needs to be indicated first on the form. _____

_____

2   Which categories of description ask you to check a box? _____

_____

3   Which categories of description ask you to write details? _____

_____

_____

4   Which questions require you to describe what you saw? _____

_____

_____

5   Which question asks you to guess or estimate? _____

_____

Discoveries

1   Describe your own complexion. _____

_____

2   Add descriptive words to the list below. Use different words from those in the form.

Appearance	Demeanor
smartly dressed, unkempt	confident, shifty

Delving More Deeply

1   What is the purpose of this form?

_____

_____

2   How do the check box sections simplify the description? _____

_____

3   Why do you think the sex, height, build, and hair color are established first?

_____

4   Why are tattoos/scars included later in the description? _____

_____

Hidden Depths

1   If you have witnessed a suspicious incident, fill in the form detailing what you remember. If not, fill in the suspicious person section describing a famous fictional "bad guy." Share and discuss.

2   Draw a picture of a person. Exchange pictures with a partner, and write a detailed description of your partner's picture.

_____

_____

_____

Extend Yourself

•   Write an account of a suspicious incident from the point of view of an innocent bystander. Then write the incident from the point of view of the offender.

•   Sketch and label the scene of the incident, including where you stood.

•   Pretend you are a police officer. What additional questions could you ask the witness?

•   Write up a role play of a suspicious incident; then perform it.

•   With a partner, write a news report on a fictional incident. Include a headline, picture, caption, and informative report. Format your report on the computer.

LESSON (33) **An Unhappy Customer**

Cross-Curriculum Literacy Links: Civics and Citizenship; Work, Employment and Enterprise

Text Type	Letter of complaint
Purpose	To communicate information, experiences, or ideas, formally or informally, in writing, to a reader who is not present
Structure	**1** Address and date
	2 Greeting or salutation
	3 Series of events or issues in paragraphs
	4 Closing and signature
Features	Set layout, informal or formal language depending on purpose and audience, varied sentences

Caring for Citizens Charity

119 S. First Street, Suite 3
Mulberry City, AL 23456

Jan. 29, 2007

Dear Mr. Jespersen:

I would first like to say that I appreciate and admire the work that Caring for Citizens does in our city and our country. It is good to know that people in need have a place to turn for food, shelter, and counseling. Caring for Citizens is a vital part of our city, and I have been glad to volunteer and donate to the charity in the past.

However, today I must write to complain about a problem. We recently bought a new refrigerator and wanted to donate our used model to Caring for Citizens. I spoke with an office worker at the charity and explained that the used model is clean and in good working condition and will see someone through many more years of service.

The office worker agreed that Caring for Citizens could easily find a family in need of a good refrigerator and instructed me to leave the unit outside our home for pick-up on Thursday, January 14. She said that a truck would come by to pick it up. But by the end of the day Thursday, no truck had come.

My wife and I had to load the fridge onto a dolly and lug it back into the garage. The next day, I called the office again, received an apology, and was told to take the fridge back outside. I did this, but again, no one came by to pick the unit up. On this day, we had rain; so not only did we have to bring the unit back inside for a second time, we also had to clean it.

I called the office again, but I was only able to leave a message, to which no one has responded.

I would still like to donate this good machine to Caring for Citizens. I will arrange to have the unit outside on February 2. If Caring for Citizens does not come by to pick it up on that day, I will be forced to choose another charity to receive this valuable donation. Please contact me at the number on the letterhead to confirm this pick-up date.

Yours sincerely,

Sam McKay

On the Surface

1 What is the complainant's name? _____
_____

2 What does Mr. McKay want to do? _____
_____

3 What problem does Mr. McKay report? _____
_____
_____

4 What is the name of the charity? _____
_____

5 What does Mr. McKay want the charity to do? _____
_____

Discoveries

1 What nouns does the writer use to refer to the refrigerator he wants to donate?
_____

2 Which of these words is formal? Informal? Which words are general rather than specific?
_____

Delving More Deeply

1 Why does Mr. McKay begin his letter of complaint with a compliment?
_____
_____

2 What do you think Mr. McKay expected when he called the office on Friday, Jan. 15?
_____
_____

3 What does Mr. McKay hope the charity will do after picking up the refrigerator?
_____

4 What does Mr. McKay say he will do if the unit is not picked up on Feb. 2?
_____

Hidden Depths

1   Have you ever volunteered to work with a charitable group? What work do volunteers do?

_____

_____

_____

2   Why is a letter a more powerful way to voice a complaint than a simple phone call? When might you write a letter of complaint, and to whom?

_____

_____

_____

Extend Yourself

•   Take the role of Mr. Jespersen and write a reply to Mr. McKay.

•   Find out what charities operate in your area and what kinds of donations they need. Offer to design a flyer to distribute at local stores, alerting the community to the charity's needs and services.

•   Locate a problem in your community — the city park that is never mowed, the sidewalks that need repair — and write a polite letter of complaint to the person or office who can attend to the problem.

LESSON 34 # Tickle the Taste Buds

Cross-Curriculum Literacy Links: Multicultural Content; Health; Geography

Text Type Menu
Purpose To display available food choices
Structure 1 List of courses in order of service
2 Details of dishes in each course outlined
Features Technical language relating to ingredients and food preparation

Round-the-World Dinner Party

Hors-d'oeuvres: Asia
Vegetable rice paper rolls (Vietnam)
Samosas (India)
Spring rolls (China)
Sushi (Japan)

Entrée: Middle East
Hummus and eggplant dips with bread
Grape leaves, stuffed
Fried cheese

Main: Europe
Coq au Vin (France)
Beef Wellington (England)
Roast vegetables
Brussels sprouts, bacon,
    squash & cracked pepper

Dessert: U.S.A.
Pecan pie
Bombe Alaska
Cherry pie

On the Surface

1 How many courses are there on this menu? _____

_____

2 List the countries from which the hors-d'oeuvres come. _____

_____

3 Which course serves pies? _____

_____

4 Which course serves a lot of vegetables? _____

_____

5 Which course lists a country rather than a region? _____

_____

Discoveries

1 **a** Find out the meanings of the words below.

  hors-d'oeuvres _____

  entrée _____

   b Make a list of other foods which fit into these categories.

_____

2 Find two other words from a language other than English used for referring to food or drinks in recipes.

_____

Delving More Deeply

1 Which course is more likely to be served before guests move to the dinner table?

_____

2 Which other course on the menu might be shared with others?

_____

3 Which direction around the world are the diners proceeding as they go from course to course?

_____

4 If one of the guests were vegetarian, which dishes could he or she eat?

_____

_____

Hidden Depths

1 List the foods on this menu you have not tried before. List the foods that you would really like to eat. Which wouldn't you eat? Why?

_____

_____

_____

2 The menu is very extensive. Which courses may be skipped? Explain.

_____

_____

_____

Extend Yourself

- The menu stops in the U.S.A. Make up another dinner party menu of your own for the remainder of the journey. Include Central America, South America, Africa, Australia and the Pacific. You will need to find out the sort of foods people typically eat in these areas.

- Create a dinner menu for you and your friends with your favorite foods listed. Place in brackets the countries these dishes come from. On a map, plot your culinary journey.

- Create a vegetarian or low-fat menu for your guests.

- Make a list of foods you know are traditionally eaten with your hands.

- Find out more about how food is served in different cultures. For example, in some cultures food is served in the center of the table for everyone to share; in some cultures salad is served after the main course. Write a report on any interesting traditions, outlining the country or cultures which follow this practice.

LESSON 35 # Cooking for Friends

Cross-Curriculum Literacy Links: Multicultural Content; Health; Geography; Mathematics

Text Type	Instructions/Procedure
Purpose	To give instructions or show how something is accomplished through a series of steps
Structure	1 Opening statement of goal or aim
	2 Material required listed in order of use
	3 Series of steps listed in chronological order
Features	Logical sequence of steps; may use technical language

Fried Rice

Serves 4
Cooking time: 10 mins
Preparation time: 20 mins

1 cup small prawns, cooked and chopped
¼ cup peas
I cup ham, chopped
1 onion, chopped
¼ cup bacon bits
2 eggs
3 green onions, chopped
2 tablespoons soy sauce
1⅓ cups cooked rice (store in fridge)
3 tablespoons oil

1 Lightly beat the two eggs. Pour a little oil into the wok and cook the eggs as an omelette. Take the omelette out and put aside.
2 Place more oil in the wok and add the onion and bacon bits, stir until onion is transparent. Add ham and cook for another minute.
3 Add the peas (pre-cooked or frozen) and rice. Stir-fry for 4 minutes. The rice should be heated all the way through and be slightly golden.
4 Cut the omelette into thin strips and add to the mixture. Add the chopped green onion, soy sauce and prawns. Cook for an additional minute. Serve.

On the Surface

1 Which ingredient needs to be pre-cooked and stored in the fridge? _____
_____

2 How long are the peas cooked for? _____
_____

3 How many people does this recipe serve? _____
_____

4 How many eggs are in the omelette? _____
_____

5 How much preparation time is required? _____

Discoveries

1 Find out what the following abbreviations in recipes stand for.

   a 2 tsp   _____

   b ½ C   _____

   c 1 tbsp   _____

2 Put the following in order from the smallest amount to the largest: cup, teaspoon, pinch, tablespoon, quart, gallon.
_____

Delving More Deeply

1 Does the preparation time include the time needed to cook and refrigerate the rice?
_____

2 List the ingredients that need to be prepared before cooking. Which would you do first? Why?
_____
_____

3 Why do you think the omelette is added to the dish only at the end? _____
_____

4 Which ingredients in this recipe would require further knowledge as to how to cook them?

_____

5 Why do you think the bacon bits and onion are the first ingredients to be cooked in the wok?

_____

Hidden Depths

1 Did you find the recipe easy to follow? Does it inspire you to cook this dish? Which foods do we tend to buy and not cook ourselves? Why?

_____

_____

_____

2 You can add or remove parts of this recipe. What would you add to or remove from the ingredients to make your own version of fried rice? What else would you serve as an accompanying dish to fried rice?

_____

_____

_____

Extend Yourself

- Get permission to try out the recipe for fried rice. Bring the dish to class and have a taste test.
- Find out how long it takes to cook different kinds of rice, and create a recipe for one kind.
- Demonstrate how to make fried rice for your class.
- With a partner, prepare an oral presentation about dishes using rice from different countries. On a map, show which countries use rice as a staple food.

Main Idea Web

Details
_____
_____
_____

Details
_____
_____
_____

Main Idea
_____
_____
_____
_____

Details
_____
_____
_____

Details
_____
_____
_____

Details
_____
_____
_____

Details
_____
_____
_____

Main Idea
_____
_____
_____
_____

Details
_____
_____
_____

Details
_____
_____
_____

NAME _____ DATE _____

Story Map

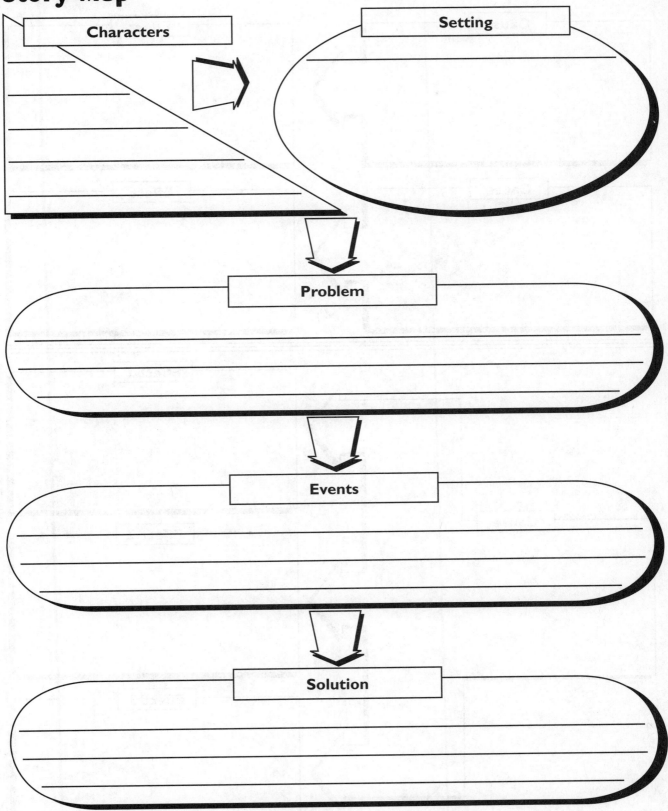

Characters

Setting

Problem

Events

Solution

Reading Comprehension Across the Genres 7, SV 1419023624

Cause and Effect Charts

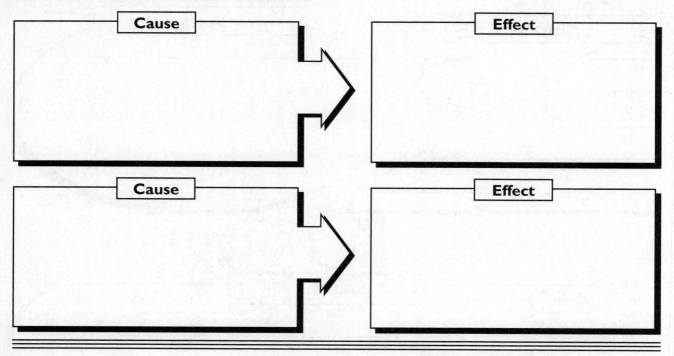

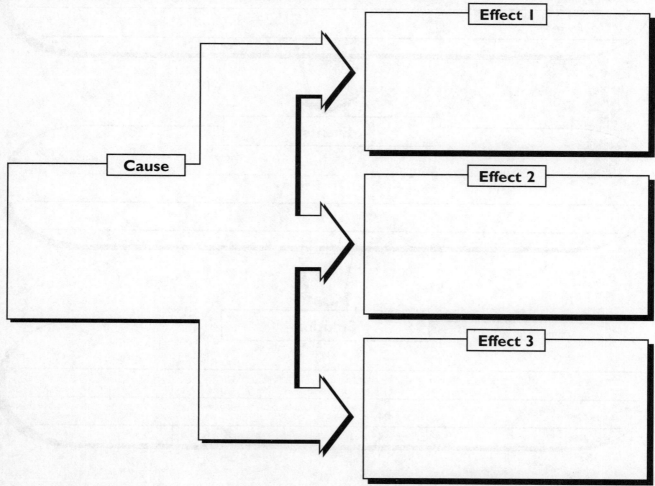

Graphic Organizers: Cause and Effect Charts
Reading Comprehension Across the Genres 7, SV 1419023624

Venn Diagram

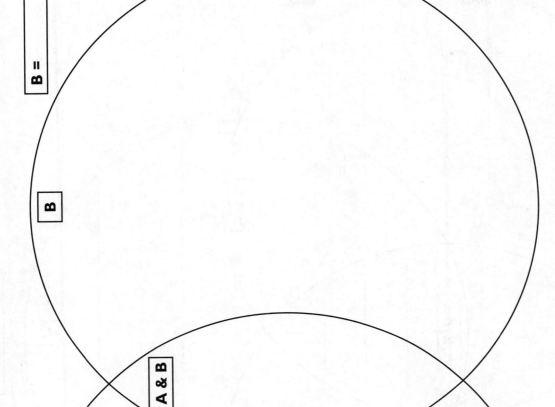

Venn Diagram

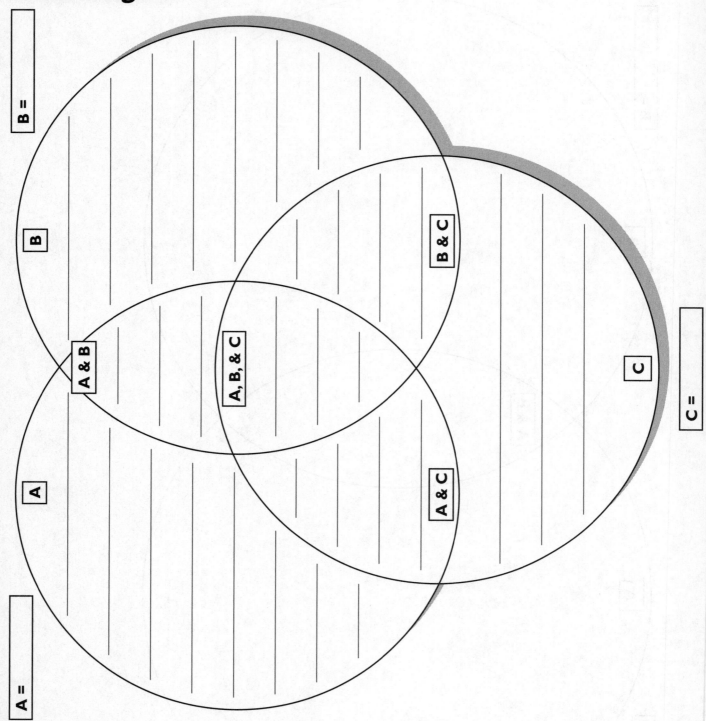

B =

B

B & C

A & B

A, B, & C

C

A

A & C

C =

A =

Word Web

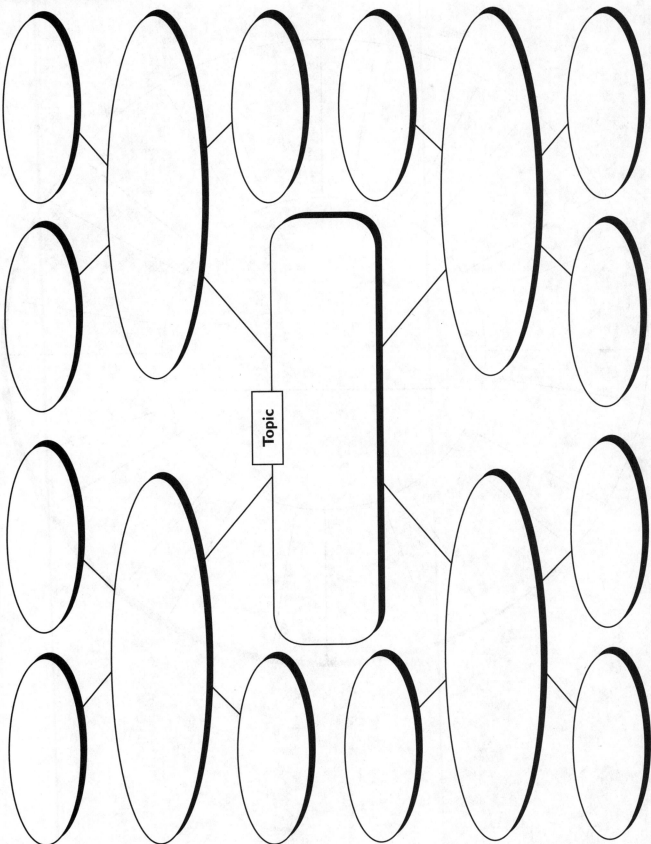

Topic

Word Wheel

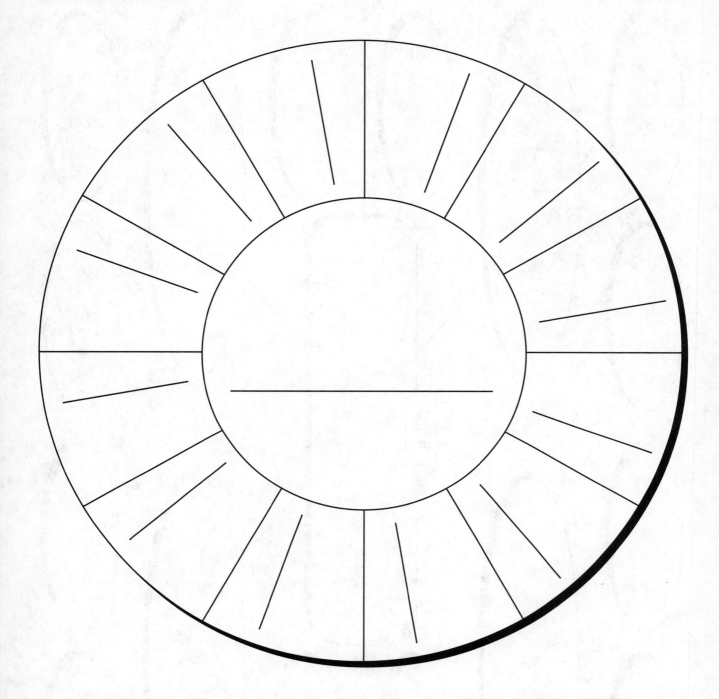

Reading Comprehension Across the Genres, Grade 7
Answer Key

Lesson 1, pages 9–11

On the Surface
1. Aldridge, Tertzowjic
2. Luke Aldridge's
3. He doesn't have the key.
4. They all knew what they would find.

Discoveries
1. **a.** main
   b. the leader of a school
   c. a play featuring exaggerated acting and emotions
   d. hesitated
   e. doubtful
   f. moved quickly
   g. bent over
2. "pounding the old wooden floorboards like hammers"; "like animals in a field"
3. No; their not knowing creates suspense and interest.

Delving More Deeply
1. They put their heads down.
2. The writer seems to have sympathy for the boys because of how he describes the Deputy Principal as unattractive, mean, and conceited.
3. No, the Deputy Principal calls it "your" case (to Aldridge), but Tertzowjic has the key, so ownership is unclear.
4. The text says Aldridge is nervous, and his movements are clumsy as he works the dial on the combination lock.
5. Responses will vary.

Hidden Depths
1. Responses will vary.
2. Responses will vary.

Lesson 2, pages 12–14

On the Surface
1. Munich and Bistritz
2. 8:35 P.M., May 1st
3. train
4. chicken and red pepper
5. b

Discoveries
1. Share and discuss.
2. **a.** quick look, glance
   b. idea, feeling
   c. excellent, wonderful
   d. darkness, evening
   e. hot, spicy
   f. spare time
   g. small amount
   h. far

Delving More Deeply
1. English and German
2. c
3. by visiting the British Museum in London and doing some research
4. train travel, style of language, research at British Museum, visiting a nobleman

Hidden Depths
1. Jonathan's girlfriend or wife; he thinks about her often; he wants to get a recipe for her
2. Responses will vary; excited, interested, weary, a little nervous due to long journey and traveling into unknown situation, but looking forward to adventure

Lesson 3, pages 15–17

On the Surface
1. on the farm
2. They walked for 20 minutes.
3. father, grandmother, cousins
4. biting, kicking, hitting, crying
5. a home for Aboriginal children who were considered "white enough" to go to school and have an education

Discoveries
1. He is taken away from his family and told to forget them.
2. It means the process of taking people out of one culture and making them become part of another culture. In the story, people attempt to assimilate the author's father into white culture.

Delving More Deeply
1. They saw their mothers screaming and crying and knew something bad was going to happen.
2. They saw the looks on the men's faces.
3. that he had a family
4. He finished high school at the top of his class.

Hidden Depths
1. Responses will vary. For example: Shocked, numb, angry, scared, sad
2. Responses will vary.

Lesson 4, pages 18–20

On the Surface
1. in the nations bounded by the Indian Ocean
2. A tsunami devastated their coastal regions.
3. on December 26, 2004
4. food, water, medicine, supplies for rebuilding
5. quickly and generously

Discoveries
1. **a.** gifts of goods such as blankets and clothing
   b. concern; care
   c. isolation; distance
2. Dear Sir or Dear Madam
3. They might write their full name, just their first name, or they might use a pseudonym (such as "Angry in Arizona") or ask to have their name withheld.

Delving More Deeply
1. They feel sympathy for the victims and a human kinship with them; it makes them feel good to be able to help.
2. to follow up on gifts and encourage charities and politicians to make sure that the aid reaches those who need it
3. Distance, lack of transportation, committee disputes in organizations, and political unrest are obstacles to getting the aid to the people.
4. She is impressed and moved by their generosity.

Hidden Depths
1. Responses will vary.
2. Responses will vary.

Lesson 5, pages 21–23

On the Surface
1. six
2. two
3. the word *privacy*
4. the word *prize* and superscript number 1

Discoveries
1. Responses will vary.
2. *private*

Delving More Deeply
1. toilets
2. lawyer, priest, minister, doctor
3. privatization
4. privacy

Hidden Depths
1. Responses will vary.
2. Responses will vary.

Lesson 6, pages 24–26

On the Surface
1. Three of them are animals rather than humans.
2. Frankie, a dog, and Muffin and Slinky, cats, are the pets of a man named Jimmy.
3. They have to rub against his legs to remind him to feed them.
4. to the park to play catch
5. All three are male. They refer to each other using the words *he, Mr.,* and *guys.*

Discoveries
1. **a.** orange-colored
   b. silly; unreasonable
   c. understand
   d. irrational fear of close spaces
   e. little bits of dry pet food
2. Frankie, Muffin, Slinky

Delving More Deeply
1. He's vain, and he thinks the name Jimmy gave him doesn't reflect his grace and beauty.
2. Slinky is happy with his life indoors and wants nothing to do with the messy world outside. Muffin is bored with indoor life and wants to try something new.
3. Frankie's lines have the most. Being a dog, he's excitable and not shy about revealing his enjoyment of life.
4. Outside, wind, dirt, and contact with children will mess up his perfectly groomed coat and whiskers.

Hidden Depths
1. Responses will vary.
2. Responses will vary.

Lesson 7, pages 27–29

On the Surface
1. friction, chemical heat, electrical heat, the sun
2. candle, matches, methylated spirits, Bunsen burner, hydrochloric acid, caustic soda
3. Focus light on the body or look at the sun.
4. Hold the back of your hand to the likely source of heat.
5. sodium hydroxide

Discoveries
1. It is a procedure used to test a hypothesis.
2. I know that it is a list of instructions to follow to establish whether the hypothesis is correct.
3. Responses will vary: numbered list; use of commands ("Put . . ." "Light . . ."), subheads; the sentence in capitals to bring the reader's attention to a warning.

Delving More Deeply
1. friction (two pieces of wood), candle, methylated spirits, Bunsen burner, magnifying glass
2. friction
3. electrical
4. friction — human energy/movement; chemical — chemical reactions; electrical — electricity; sun is a source of energy in itself

Hidden Depths
1. Responses will vary.
2. Responses will vary.

Lesson 8, pages 30–32

On the Surface
1. pools of water, polished stones, metallic objects
2. to see our reflection, to see behind us and around corners when cycling or driving
3. It travels in straight lines.
4. Shine a flashlight in a dark room.
5. hitting another surface or the eye of the observer

Discoveries
1. **a.** most beautiful
   b. mirror image
   c. shined
   d. made of or like metal
   e. supernatural
   f. pictures, impressions
   g. characteristics
   h. starting place
   i. the state of being able; capacity
2. Some or all of it bounces back.

Delving More Deeply
1. When light hits something that is blocking its path, and the light cannot pass through the object, a shadow is created.
2. that light bounces back in straight lines
3. b
4. If light bent around things, it would not be blocked off and so there would be no shadows.
5. No, shadows are created because the path of light is blocked.

Hidden Depths
1. Responses will vary.
2. Responses will vary.

Lesson 9, pages 33–35

On the Surface
1. Rocket Ship Galileo
2. the moon
3. barren wastes, mountain peaks, great gaping craters
4. Ross, Art, Cargraves, Morrie
5. The moon people did it to themselves.

Discoveries
1. **a.** emptiness
   b. lifeless
   c. terrible; horrifying
   d. metal and rock masses moving through outer space
3. doesn't make sense, doesn't stand up under careful consideration

Delving More Deeply
1. Tycho
2. b
3. They boiled away.
4. He needs to land and examine the surface closely.

Hidden Depths
1. Responses will vary.
2. Responses will vary.

Lesson 10, pages 36–38

On the Surface
1. bad person or deed, bad weather, bad conditions, bad accident, food was bad, bad smell, bad workmanship, bad business, she feels bad, sweets are bad for your teeth
2. c
3. minor, slight
4. cruel
5. foul, lousy

Discoveries
1. Responses will vary.

2.

```
T N E L O V E L A M A
Y A L U F E T A H B B
L U N G O D L Y H A O
T G O E S O B O S B M
S H L G L S R E I S I
A T U U I R R F G M N
E Y F O E N A E M E A
B W U N W O R N I L B
A G T M O S H T A I L
B D E K C I W L I V E
Q B I S L U F N I S T
```

Delving More Deeply

1. Responses will vary.
2. Responses will vary. Sample: The weather was atrocious, making driving conditions adverse and resulting in a nasty accident.
3. notorious, infamous
4. Responses will vary. Examples: naughty, unkind, unworthy; ungodly, evil, abhorrent

Hidden Depths

1. Responses will vary.
2. Responses will vary.

Lesson 11, pages 39–41

On the Surface

1. Roddy Doyle; Rover Saves Christmas; Scholastic Press; $24.95
   Lemony Snicket; The Hostile Hospital: A Series of Unfortunate Events, Book the Eighth; HarperCollins; $17.95
   Judy Sierra; Counting Crocodiles; Voyager; $16.75
2. The Giggler Treatment
3. The Bad Beginning (1), The Reptile Room (2), The Wide Window (3), The Miserable Mill (4), The Austere Academy (5), The Ersatz Elevator (6), The Vile Village (7)
4. preschoolers

Discoveries

1. **a.** taking advantage of
   b. threatening; approaching
   c. very funny
   d. pitiable
   e. very unhappy
2. poor, pathetic; Heimlich Hospital; feasting fearlessly on fishes
3. Responses will vary.

Delving More Deeply

1. Preschoolers: it's brightly illustrated and is about counting to 10.
2. She or he likes it very much and says that it is "a must" for young children.
3. On Christmas Eve, Santa's sleigh is grounded and Rudolph is sick. Can Rover, a wealthy dog who can travel at supersonic speed, save the day?
4. Responses will vary. Share and discuss.

Hidden Depths

1. Responses will vary.
2. Responses will vary.
3. in newspapers and magazines, on-line

Lesson 12, pages 42–44

On the Surface

1. among the semi-trailers at the edge of the tarmac
2. into the café with the passengers
3. two sleepy teenagers
4. the knapsack
5. to wait for a car to sweep past

Discoveries

1. **a.** very dirty
   b. lean over
   c. solitary
   d. avoided
   e. move slowly and stealthily
   f. carefully, to avoid causing pain
   g. without haste or concern
   h. casually
2. third person
3. past tense
4. travelers gathering like moths

Delving More Deeply

1. He describes her avoiding the bright lights and waiting in the shadows, while the other travelers gather in the café.
2. to find out whether the seat would be empty
3. in the middle of the night: it's dark, the passengers are yawning
4. lonely, shunned, wait, stir, creep, watch, careful, concealed, smile; nonchalantly, slipped. Her behavior is suspicious and sneaky — makes the reader wonder what she's up to.

Hidden Depths

1. Responses will vary.
2. Responses will vary.

Lesson 13, pages 45–47

On the Surface

1. a teenage boy or girl who's always running behind
2. looks for something to wear that's relatively clean
3. The school bus leaves in just twenty minutes.
4. It's just the way he or she is — it's how he or she has decided to live life.
5. There's nothing to be late for.

Discoveries

1. **a.** a cold, blended drink of fruit and yogurt or milk
   b. performing with ease
2. a-LARM wrecks my DREAMS at SEV-en THIR-ty;
   The rhythm works for the poem's main lines but not for its refrain.

Delving More Deeply

1. Responses will vary. Share and discuss.
2. Gotta, 'Cause, markin', breezin', Uh-unh, no way
3. Responses will vary. Sample: The writer is using very informal language; the writer likes the edgy look of the poem without punctuation; the writer knows that readers can figure out where ideas begin and end from the poem's line breaks and rhythm.
4. "Late is a way of life (for me)" is the main repeated phrase. It stresses the idea that lateness dominates the speaker's life and that he or she isn't likely to change soon.

Hidden Depths

1. Responses will vary.
2. Responses may vary. Sample: These lines are a kind of refrain. Perhaps they are meant to be spoken by another person or group of people, like a chorus. Perhaps the italics draw attention to their repetition.

Lesson 14, pages 48–50

On the Surface

1. They were a warrior elite.
2. the cavalry
3. Armor, equipment, war-horses
4. sons of knights
5. grooming horses, looking after armor, serving food

Discoveries

1. Responses will vary. Sample: Chivalry was the code of behavior that governed knights' lives in wartime and peace.
2. The elite are the most powerful and influential people in a society. In our society, the wealthy and politically powerful are the elite.

Delving More Deeply
1. Responses will vary.
2. special bath, dress in white, pray at altar in front of sword and armor.
   Mass, dress knight in armor, prayers said over armor and sword, knight given blow to neck by another knight, vow to act according to the code of chivalry.
3. to God
4. Conditions were often violent and unsettled, so military power was important.

Hidden Depths
1. Responses will vary.
2. Responses will vary.

Lesson 15, pages 51–53

On the Surface
1. Jesse Martin's
2. December 7, 1998
3. southeast part of Australia
4. October 31, 1999
5. twice

Discoveries
1. east
2. southern
3. Students should add the Cape of Good Hope at the southern-most tip of Africa and Cape Horn to the southernmost tip of South America.
4. the Azores
5. There is no wind, so the boat doesn't move.

Delving More Deeply
1. the main parts of his journey, detailed in his book *Lionheart*
2. 18 days
3. the Pacific
4. Responses will vary. Most likely points 16, 17: force 10 storm and no power
5. It was the mid-way point in his journey. He was half-way around the world.

Hidden Depths
1. Responses will vary.
2. Responses will vary.

Lesson 16, pages 54–56

On the Surface
1. car, bus, train
2. the number of passengers per car, bus or train; number of miles per person per gallon of fuel
3. Transportation and the Atmosphere
4. No
5. 40, 60

Discoveries
1. *Per* means "for each"; it comes from the Latin word meaning "for."
2. They use "liter" or "litre" to measure the amount of fuel and "kilometer" or "kilometre" to measure distance.

Delving More Deeply
1. 136.1 miles
2. Public transport is more fuel-efficient and therefore is better for the atmosphere.
3. have more than one passenger
4. train

Hidden Depths
1. Responses will vary.
2. Responses will vary.

Lesson 17, pages 57–59

On the Surface
1. coal-burning power plants
2. more than 66 million tons
3. Use scrubbers to clean the smoke before it comes out of the smokestacks.
4. They are costly to install.

Discoveries
1. Responses will vary.
2. Sulfur dioxide is a smelly, toxic gas that is used to make cleaners, such as bleaches, and to refrigerate things. But it is also a major air pollutant.

Delving More Deeply
1. It would cost too much.
2. ruined forests and lakes and polluted air
3. smoke mixes with fog
4. People can suffocate when they breathe it in. London, 1952
5. They built tall smokestacks so that high winds carried the smoke away.

Hidden Depths
1. Responses will vary.
2. Responses will vary.

Lesson 18, pages 60–62

On the Surface
1. Christie Devon and Mrs. Saltonstall
2. a job looking after and teaching two small children
3. Like their mother, they are overdressed, weighed down with clothing.
4. It's just been curled; touching it will mess it up.

Discoveries
1. **a.** unwell
   b. save money
   c. worried, distracted
   d. calmness
   e. alarmed
2. She is too young to say it correctly.

Delving More Deeply
1. She is willing to work cheaply because she doesn't know what salary she should ask for.
2. She is willing to exploit Christie by paying her too little, but she is not willing to give up her little luxuries to cut costs.
3. Responses will vary. Sample: They overdo everything — clothes as well as names.
4. Responses will vary. Sample: She is proud that she can afford to dress them like pretty dolls.

Hidden Depths
1. Responses will vary.
2. Responses will vary.

Lesson 19, pages 63–65

On the Surface
1. Camp SunRay — where your young athlete will shine!
2. coaches' profiles; costs and registration forms; maps to the camp
3. six
4. soccer, tennis singles and doubles, swimming, diving, and life-saving

Discoveries
1. parents' pride in their children's abilities; parents' desire to provide their children with opportunities for fun and healthy growth
2. nine times; to generate a feeling of excitement about the camp

Delving More Deeply
1. to persuade parents that with the right coaching, their children can be top performers, too
2. eight, once in the title and once per section of text; This repetition drills the camp's name into the reader's memory.
3. meeting new friends and making life-long memories
4. They may miss their children or worry that their children are homesick; or they may want to check out the camp while it's running.

Hidden Depths
1. Responses will vary.
2. Responses will vary.

Lesson 20, pages 66–68

On the Surface
1. three times the energy now generated
2. using coal, oil, and other fossil fuels
3. heat-trapping greenhouse gases
4. global warming
5. many options: improving existing technologies and developing others, such as fusion reactors, or solar-based solar plants

Discoveries
1. **a.** search
   b. use up
   c. improving the use of
   d. relying heavily on factories and machines
2. Responses will vary.

Delving More Deeply
1. the Apollo program to put a man on the moon
2. No, they require more research and development or are simply inadequate. The world's energy needs are growing.
3. No, he advocates "a quantum jump" (i.e., investing money to solve the problem sooner).
4. Industrialized countries use the most energy. Also, they have the money and the technology to make changes more easily.

Hidden Depths
1. Responses will vary.
2. Responses will vary.

Lesson 21, pages 69–71

On the Surface
1. any number
2. a kip and two coins
3. games and souvenir shops
4. The boxer was in control of the timing of the spinning of the pennies.

Discoveries
1. **a.** viewers
   b. no longer be the spinner
2. Students can define kip, boxer, and spinner.
3. to make them easier to follow, and to find any particular direction at a glance

Delving More Deeply
1. The spinner spins the coins and tries to throw heads.
2. The other players guess whether the spinner will throw heads or tails.
3. the players who guessed that the spinner would throw tails
4. Both coins need to come up heads three times in a row.
5. Keep score of how many times each player wins a round, and then take the best out of 3 or 5 rounds.

Hidden Depths
1. Responses will vary.
2. Responses will vary.

Lesson 22, pages 72–74

On the Surface
1. to feed pets a healthy diet, get pets needed shots, exercise pet, and spay or neuter pet
2. The animals can no longer produce litters of offspring.
3. They roam and get into fights over females.
4. that these procedures make animals lazy and fat

Discoveries
1. **a.** topic of concern
   b. multiple offspring
   c. to spray with a strong-smelling hormone
   d. commonly believed untruth
   e. put to death humanely
2. Spayed and neutered animals live longer and healthier lives, behave better, and do not bear litters of unwanted animals that must be euthanized. The procedures are simple, safe, and not painful.

Delving More Deeply
1. Responses will vary. Sample: They have found homes for the littermates; they think kittens or puppies are cute; they want to sell the littermates.
2. to pet owners' affection for their pets, to their sense of duty and responsibility to care for the pets they've chosen to get, and to their sympathy for unwanted animals
3. a
4. a

Hidden Depths
1. Responses will vary.
2. Some animals are bred for abilities such as hunting or traits such as intelligence. Others are bred for show. Breeders work hard to strengthen genetic traits.

Lesson 23, pages 75–77

On the Surface
1. any reader's grandfather
2. an old-timer
3. the grandfather when he was a teenager
4. the cartoonist

Discoveries
1. a story of the past that is full of exaggerated events
2. Responses will vary. An old-timer may be a comic character who is not taken seriously by listeners, or a wise character to whom listeners pay attention.

Delving More Deeply
1. No, because it is not possible for a road to go uphill both ways.
2. Probably not — this is the kind of story many older people tell to children and grandchildren.
3. He had to walk everywhere, school was three miles away, the weather was awful, and the road was steep.
4. Responses will vary.

Hidden Depths
1. Responses will vary.
2. A Möbius strip is a one-sided rectangular strip, named after a mathematician, that gives the appearance of three dimensions because it is twisted. Responses will vary to the second question. Sample: The strip may represent the twisting of history that memory sometimes causes.

Lesson 24, pages 78–80

On the Surface
1. a new food pyramid
2. Scientists know more about the body and how it uses food than they used to.
3. mypyramid.gov
4. daily exercise

Discoveries
1. **a.** eating
   b. scientists who study how our bodies use food
   c. make sense of
   d. stripped of outer coatings
   e. flaws
2. Responses will vary.

Delving More Deeply
1. It's harder to interpret than the old one; it doesn't recommend whole grains over refined grains; it uses colors rather than words.
2. It took time and money to study the latest research in nutrition, to talk to scientists, and to design a graphic that would make sense to everyone.
3. Graphics are striking and easy to remember, but it's hard to memorize many words.
4. help choosing good foods, planning a diet, and developing an exercise program

Hidden Depths
1. Responses will vary.
2. Responses will vary.

Reading Comprehension Across the Genres 7, SV 1419023624

Lesson 25, pages 81–83

On the Surface
1. put on a top, head off, stop near a favorite spot, explore/not explore bridge, sit under a tree, relax with a book, see an animal, see a house, head home
2. the one about the favorite top
3. question 5
4. next to a particular tree

Discoveries
1. **a.** outgoing
   b. full of desire to succeed
   c. understanding; concerned
   d. full of life
   e. hopeful
   f. sudden; unplanned
2. Responses will vary.

Delving More Deeply
1. how you see yourself
2. Responses will vary. Sample: Choose the one you do most often.
3. Responses will vary. Sample: People carry their things in bags; bags are useful, have a purpose. They symbolize being organized, practical, or spontaneous.
4. Responses will vary. Sample: how adventurous you are

Hidden Depths
1. Responses will vary.
2. Responses will vary.

Lesson 26, pages 84–86

On the Surface
1. Language Arts is much longer than the other classes.
2. two male teachers, four female teachers; no, because you can't tell whether the coaches are male or female
3. a
4. Three are mentioned — A Wing, B Wing, and C Wing.

Discoveries
1. **a.** Responses will vary.
   b. Responses will vary.
   c. Responses will vary.
   d. Responses will vary.
2. Ms., Mr., days of the week, lang., stud., PE, bldg. These abbreviations save room and give the chart a clean, easy-to-read look.

Delving More Deeply
1. social studies
2. Ms. Fife
3. It might be raining outside, or the team might be working on strength training rather than practicing.
4. PE is a subject in which all students exercise and play various sports. It is scheduled separately from tennis, a specific sport that not everyone chooses to play.

Hidden Depths
1. Language arts and math are daily classes because they provide the foundation for success in all other classes.
2. Responses will vary.

Lesson 27, pages 87–89

On the Surface
1. Heads of Port Phillip Bay
2. Jesse's boat
3. 14
4. Sunday, December 7, 1998
5. what he learned from the experience

Discoveries
1. **a.** opened; unrolled
   b. turned aside from
   c. conclusion; end
   d. often used; trite
2. It signifies courage and strength.

Delving More Deeply
1. Responses will vary.
2. his parents
3. his family background, along with what happened on his journey and what he learned from the experience
4. his comments in the diary about how *Lionheart* might prefer to stay home
5. They thought he was a foolish young man.

Hidden Depths
1. Responses will vary.
2. Responses will vary.

Lesson 28, pages 90–92

On the Surface
1. the United States
2. Linda Sue Park's book, *A Single Shard*
3. Read Any Good Books Lately?
4. 57
5. Add your own comments; recommend a book similar to this one.

Discoveries
1. **a.** an adult who cares for a child
   b. a broken piece of pottery
   c. risking
2. 4 replaces the word for, and 2 replaces the word to.
3. Responses will vary. Sample: overuse of exclamation marks; use of "4ever" and "2" for "to"; casual vocabulary

Delving More Deeply
1. a novel about a boy finding his place in the world
2. It is set in Korea and involves a boy whose father has died but who finds other father-figures who help him achieve his dreams.
3. It's easy to access and update as new books come out, and it's free for readers.
4. 9–13
5. the characters, the emotions

Hidden Depths
1. Responses will vary.
2. Responses will vary.

Lesson 29, pages 93–95

On the Surface
1. Ovation (Channel 43), Hallmark (Channel 24), Nickelodeon (Channel 5), Cartoon Network (Channel 28), Disney (Channel 27), BBC World (Channel 37)
2. the evening sessions are highlighted
3. 3; Nickelodeon, Cartoon Network, Disney
4. every hour
5. They all do.

Discoveries
1. parental guidance suggested
2. G–general audience, PG13–parental guidance suggested for children under 13; M–for mature audiences only

Delving More Deeply
1. travel, business, Asia, sport, environment, computers
2. British Broadcasting Company
3. The channel shows programs, such as The Lion King, for all members of the family, not just children.
4. Ovation, 43

Hidden Depths
1. Responses will vary.
2. Responses will vary.

Lesson 30, page 96–98

On the Surface
1. *Holes*, directed by Andrew Davis
2. Louis Sachar
3. close cooperation between writer and director; actors who get into their roles; an effective score

4. Sigourney Weaver, Jon Voight, Tim Blake Nelson, Patricia Arquette, Shia LaBeouf

Discoveries
1. young moviegoers and film renters, especially those who enjoyed the novel *Holes*
2. Class discussion
3. Class discussion

Delving More Deeply
1. the Warden, Mr. Sir, and Mr. Pendanski
2. It's set in the desert, so heat, dust, and lack of cities nearby probably provided many challenges to the cast and crew.
3. She was afraid that it would be too different from the book.
4. Viewing the scenes set in the desert made the reviewer feel thirsty.

Hidden Depths
1. Responses will vary.
2. Perhaps the book's plot is too long or too complex to squeeze into a film. Perhaps the director wants to focus on the main plot and cut subplots. Perhaps there isn't enough money to hire enough actors to portray every character.

Lesson 31, pages 99–101

On the Surface
1. director Andrew Davis and writer Louis Sachar
2. He's a journalist and director who grew up in a family of actors.
3. in the west Texas desert
4. Quotation marks are used for their words.

Discoveries
1. The quotations give the article a feeling of authority and expertise, and readers have a sense of Sachar's and Davis's own ideas.
2. It makes the phrase stand out more so that readers will pay attention to it and remember it.

Delving More Deeply
1. He loved the story, and so did his children. The story is "heartfelt" and "intelligent."
2. They are evidence that writing is hard work that takes many attempts to get right.
3. A novel tells a story through words, while a screenplay tells a story through images.
4. Responses will vary. Sample: He means that the story treats kids as fully human, with the full range of human emotions, needs, and dreams. It doesn't baby kids by avoiding tough subjects, either.

Hidden Depths
1. Responses will vary.
2. Share and discuss.

Lesson 32, pages 102–104

On the Surface
1. date, time, location, and what did you witness
2. build, hair color, hair style, eye color, complexion, facial hair
3. height, hair color, facial hair, clothing, tattoo/scars, have you seen this person before
4. what did you witness, clothing, tattoo/scars, have you seen this person before
5. height

Discoveries
1. Responses will vary.
2. Responses will vary.

Delving More Deeply
1. to give details of what was witnessed and a description of the person involved
2. cuts down on the options, have to make a simpler decision
3. These are the most basic characteristics to help build an image.
4. These are finer details, added once the overall description is established.

Hidden Depths
1. Share and discuss.
2. Responses will vary.

Lesson 33, pages 105–107

On the Surface
1. Sam McKay
2. donate a refrigerator to a charity
3. Twice, the organization has failed to pick up the refrigerator when they said they would.
4. Caring for Citizens
5. to pick up the fridge without fail on Feb. 2

Discoveries
1. refrigerator, fridge, unit, machine
2. *Refrigerator* is formal; *fridge* is informal; *unit* and *machine* are both general.

Delving More Deeply
1. He wants to be civil and polite and thinks of this problem as an exception to the charity's usual efficient way of handling business.
2. He expected an apology for the inconvenience the missed pick-up caused and a quick remedy to the problem.
3. They will give it to a family who needs one but can't afford to buy one.
4. He will donate it to a different charity.

Hidden Depths
1. Responses will vary.
2. A letter takes more time to compose and send, so it sends the message that the issue is very important to the writer. Responses to second question will vary.

Lesson 34, pages 108–110

On the Surface
1. four
2. Vietnam, India, China, Japan
3. dessert
4. the main course
5. dessert

Discoveries
1. a. appetizers, main course
   b. Responses will vary.
2. Responses will vary.

Delving More Deeply
1. hors-d'oeuvres
2. Responses will vary.
3. west
4. Responses will vary. Possible choices include samosa, rice paper rolls, hummus and bread, grape leaves, roast vegetables, dessert.

Hidden Depths
1. Responses will vary.
2. Responses will vary.

Lesson 35, pages 111–113

On the Surface
1. the rice
2. four minutes
3. four
4. two
5. 20 minutes

Discoveries
1. a. 2 teaspoons
   b. one-half of a cup
   c. one tablespoon
2. pinch, teaspoon, tablespoon, cup, quart, gallon

Delving More Deeply
1. No.
2. rice, chopped green onions, chopped onion, chopped ham, cooked and chopped prawns. Do the rice first because it takes the longest.

3. It would get overcooked otherwise.
4. rice, prawns, eggs
5. They take the longest to cook.

Hidden Depths
1. Responses will vary.
2. Responses will vary.

Acknowledgments

The authors and publisher gratefully credit or acknowledge permission to reproduce extracts from the following sources:

ACP Syndication, "The True You" from *Dolly Magazine*, December 2002, ACP Publishing: Sydney, 2002. Reproduced by courtesy of Dolly Magazine; Allen & Unwin: St Leonards, 1994, map and text from *Lionheart: A Journey of the Human Spirit* by Jesse Martin with Ed Gannon (ed.), Allen & Unwin: St. Leonards, 2000; *Foxtel*, "Cable TV" abbreviated from Foxtel Magazine December 2002, ACP Publishing: Sydney: 2000; Gareth Stevens Inc., Reprinted with permission from *The Acid Rain Hazard* by Judith Woodburn. Copyright © 1992 by Gareth Stevens, Inc. All rights reserved; Harcourt Inc., "Counting Crocodiles" by Judy Sierra from "The Age Summer Book Guide" *The Age*: Melbourne, November 2001; Hodder & Stoughton Ltd., *The World of the Medieval Knight* by Christopher Gravett, Hodder Children's Books: London, 1993. Reproduced by permission of Hodder & Stoughton Limited; The Australian Student's Thesaurus by Anne Knight (ed.) © 1991 Oxford University Press, <www.oup.com.au>; Pan Macmillan, "Rocketship Galileo" by Robert Heinlein from Classic Science Fiction by Peter Haining (ed.), Macmillan: London, 1995; Pearson Education Australia, *The World of Science*, Book 2, 2nd ed. by David Heffernan and Mark Learmonth, Longman Cheshire: Melbourne, 1992; Kathleen Priest, "My Dad" by Kathleen Priest from *Nothing Interesting About Cross Street* edited by Beth Yahp, Angus & Robertson: Sydney 1996; University of Queensland Press, *Crossfire* by James Moloney, University of Queensland Press: St. Lucia, 1992 and *A Bridge to Wiseman's Cove* by James Moloney, University of Queensland Press: St. Lucia, 1996.

Every attempt has been made to trace and acknowledge copyright holders. Where the attempt has been unsuccessful, the publisher welcomes information that would redress the situation.